The power of

PURPOSE

is the key to the
"success habit"—finding, developing
and understanding the
purposeful goals that will bring
you the achievements
you most desire. In 39 brilliant
chapters—and eight practical
"exercises"—Mack R. Douglas
shares with you the proven methods
that have brought incredible success
to thousands of men and women
in all fields of life.

HOW TO MAKE A
HABIT OF SUCCEEDING

Mack R. Douglas

**ZONDERVAN
PUBLISHING HOUSE**
OF THE ZONDERVAN CORPORATION
GRAND RAPIDS, MICHIGAN 49506

HOW TO MAKE A HABIT OF SUCCEEDING
Copyright © 1966 by Zondervan Publishing House

Library of Congress Catalog Card Number 66-13694

Zondervan Publishing House edition published June 1966
Zondervan Books edition published March 1968

Twenty-second printing November 1980

ISBN 0-310-23862-5

Acknowledgment

Gratitude is expressed to the National Council of Churches of Christ for
permission to quote from the Revised Standard Version of the Bible,
copyright © 1946 and 1952 by the Division of Christian Education of the
National Council of Churches of Christ.

ZONDERVAN BOOKS are published by Zondervan Publishing House, 1415
Lake Drive, S.E., Grand Rapids, Michigan 49506, U.S.A.

Printed in the United States of America

DEDICATED
TO

Aline, Linda, Don, Laura and Elaine who now understand why those hundreds of hours late at night in the home study.

Nell Seaver and Eunice Pitcher for excellence in manuscript preparation.

Napoleon Hill, Dale Carnegie and Earl Nightingale for their influence on me and this book.

The Fort Lauderdale Sales and Marketing Executives Club for encouragement and challenge.

Walter Dunn and the staff of WFTL in Fort Lauderdale, Florida, for both the name of this book and for daring with Bob Watson and KGNC of Amarillo, Texas, to pioneer in my radio program, "How to Make a Habit of Succeeding."

FOREWORD

Success has an evasive nature that does not permit its easy acquisition by the majority of those who pursue its rewards. But success, when realized, is sweeter because of its very nature—its constant elusiveness.

Success is a montage of exceptional effort, formative planning, consistent study and circumstances over which we often have little or no control. Throughout the ages man has attempted to determine the proper combination of these factors—to assure for himself the rewards that success represents. If, perchance, one individual could create this magic combination of factors, there would be no success possible—except for those who deviated from that pattern.

Success is not made for the masses, but rather for that select few who diligently combine and recombine an endless flow of patterns into one productive process that accomplishes successful results, yet whose composition is everchanging.

Mack Douglas does not attempt to provide a format for success, but rather he gives us avenues of pursuit, elements of thinking, actions and formulas derived from experience so that we can, in our finite ability, search out, combine and develop our own design of accomplishment.

Thus, Mack Douglas can never take credit for the success of anyone who reads this book—and he does not desire to claim the credit—but he can, and will, materially contribute to the ingredients of your success. Having fortified your determination with the contents of this book, you can accomplish that success in its fullest dimension with justified pride in personal accolades.

W. HEARTSILL WILSON

CONTENTS

PART ONE
THE POWER OF PURPOSE

1. DYNAMIC PURPOSE

YOUR KEY to personal success is building a dynamic purpose. Purpose differs from goals, for purpose is like the pot of gold at the end of the rainbow—the ideal that we seek. As soon as we attain one mountain peak of purpose we see another, and another is still ahead of us. Disraeli has said that "the secret of success is constancy to purpose."

Your key for personal success today is having a high purpose.

> If you can't be a pine on the top of the hill
> Be a shrub in the valley but be
> The best little shrub by the side of the hill;
> Be a bush if you can't be a tree.
>
> If you can't be a bush be a bit of grass
> And some highway happier make;
> If you can't be a muskie then just be a bass,
> But be the liveliest bass in the lake.
>
> We can't all be captains, we've got to be crew,
> There is something for all of us. There
> Is big work to do and there's lesser to do
> And the task we must do is the near.
>
> If you can't be a highway then just be a trail;
> If you can't be the sun be a star;
> It isn't by size that you win or you fail.
> Be the best of whatever you are.
> —Douglas Malloch.[1]

When Moses stood at the burning bush God said to him, "Draw not nigh hither: put off thy shoes from off thy

---

[1]Douglas Malloch, "Be the Best of Whatever You Are," from *The Best Loved Poems of the American People* (Garden City, N.Y.: Garden City Publishing Company, 1936), page 102.

feet for the place whereon thou standest is holy ground."
Challenged by the burning bush experience Moses not only
set free 2,000,000 of his kin and countrymen but led them
through miraculous experiences for forty years to make a
nation of dedicated people out of former slaves. Today
Christians and Jews alike claim Moses to be one of the
greatest men who ever lived. He had high purpose.

Presidential Purpose

Several years ago it was my privilege to have a forty-
five minute interview with former President Harry S.
Truman. I asked him what we can do today to combat
juvenile delinquency. His answer was firm, forthright and
forceful: "Pick out their grandparents." Mr. Truman
turned to the pictures of his two grandfathers on the wall
behind the desk and related his warmhearted conviction of
what those pioneer settlers meant to his life. "I could not
be untrue to my parents and grandparents, to my family
tradition." Mr. Truman went on further to say that parents should stay out of taverns, and should take their
children to Sunday school and church and lead them in
constructive play.

Later I had the privilege of taking eighty young people
to visit Mr. Truman's library in Independence, Missouri, to
hear Mr. Truman lecture on government. Those young
people saw firsthand an excellent example of a man of
high purpose. That's the best formula I know to rid our
nation of juvenile delinquency. Give them family loyalty.
This will make a tremendous difference in their lives.

Hitler's Selfish Purpose

High purpose of course deals in the value of human
life, in the happiness of others, in lifting up the downtrodden, bringing courage to the disheartened. Earl Nightingale tells in one of his radio addresses of the German
Sixth Army at Stalingrad, composed of twenty-six divi-
sions, 300,000 well-trained, experienced troops. They were
surrounded in November of 1942 by the Russians. Instead
of allowing them to retreat from the terrible Russian
winter Hitler demanded that they stay and fight. Without
adequate supplies, without adequate ammunition and support and certainly without adequate clothing and food, by
February 200,000, or two-thirds, of these troops had been

killed, wounded or captured. More than 100,000 were killed. Of the 90,000 survivors captured by the Russians only 6,000 ever reached Germany alive. There was no high purpose in Hitler's dreams—only selfish, sordid, sick, personal ambition.

In sharp contrast look what the British army did at Dunkirk. Every possible ship, boat, raft—anything that would float—at tremendous sacrifice, was not only offered to the British General Staff but volunteered, and some even piloted by women and children. They shuttled back and forth across the channel under constant air attack until by June 3, three-fourths of the British army had been safely evacuated to Britain, living to fight again. That's the difference. The British General Staff valued human life.

In establishing high purpose you must find a great human need, find the answer to fill that need, and burn all your bridges behind you taking the answer of that need through a channel of service to the people who need it.

Purpose Comes from Within

One of the real fallacies of our day is the popular notion that happiness depends on external circumstances and surroundings. There is no question that our internal moods are colored by external situations, but real personal joy comes from internal conviction, determined by character that is the direct result of high purpose.

Success is his who is consistently progressing toward a worthy purpose. Carlyle has said, "A man with a half volition goes backwards and forwards, and makes no way on the smoothest road; a man with a whole volition advances on the roughest, and will reach his purpose, if there be even a little worthiness in it. The man without a purpose is like a ship without a rudder—a waif, a nothing, a no man. Have a purpose in life and having it, throw such strength of mind and muscle into your work as God has given you."

Peace Corps Purpose

In the spring of 1963 I saw firsthand in Northern Luzon in the Philippines some of America's most outstanding young people giving of themselves in every possible and imaginable difficult task. These were Peace Corps members, nearly 700 of them in the Philippines in all, living in thatched-roof barrios, eating the food of the Philippines, working for $2.00 a day. What drove them?

It was the high purpose expressed in the inaugural address of President John F. Kennedy when he said, "Ask not what your country can do for you, but what you can do for your country."

The man with purpose does not sit back waiting for Dame Fortune to appear, but rather, he will take every opportunity and use it to the good of others and to his own advancement.

The Path of Purpose

In accomplishing the life-long majestic adventure of high purpose you must take time to map this glorious journey. Remember when you were a child and played the games of make-believe? There were no limitations of criticism. You could do or be whatever your imagination created.

Believe it or not, steadfast dreams do come true. I dare you to be different, to leave mediocrity, one of America's greatest menaces, and travel on the high road of glorious adventure.

"See yourself as you want to be; know you can reach the level to which you aspire and, through the 'I will' spirit build upon the premise yet to be described, take the simple steps necessary to bring your plans into fruition." —Ben Sweetland.[2]

Ben Sweetland has also suggested some of the objectives you might have in your life. Under the category "Material Possessions" there might be: a new home, fine furniture, new automobile, big wardrobe, and financial security. Under "Physical Being" you might have: better health, loss of or more weight, better memory, concentration, the ability to relax, the master of habit, happiness and peace of mind. In "Public Affairs" you dream of: respect of all, leadership, a prestige job, and the love and respect of your family.

To those we would add "Spiritual Goals": a personal relationship with the Lord, the assurance of inward peace, freedom from guilt, fear and worry, strong self-confidence, the joy of service where you worship, and the

---

[2]Ben Sweetland, *I Will* (Englewood Cliffs, N.J.: Prentice-Hall, Inc., 1960), page 12.

happiness of being a worthy example to your children, friends, and associates.

How is your life? Are you on the high road of magical purpose? Then start right now. Establish a high and lofty purpose. You can be successful.

2. LIMITATIONS OF PURPOSE

YOUR KEY to personal success for today is purpose.

There are two limitations of purpose: (1) The tendency to change your purpose short of its realization, and (2) the dangers of uncontrolled ambition—uncontrolled and unguided purpose.

Changed Purpose

Have you ever seen a salesman become tremendously successful in a certain venture? Then as he gets into a larger income bracket he suddenly finds he wants to be in management or he wants to change products or he wants to go into a different field. In the process he nullifies or violates the principles and practices that brought him his success. Thus purpose is short-circuited by change in plans. The unfamiliarity of the new responsibility can often destroy the very principles that made him successful.

A singer may become successful and have a gold record in recording and nationwide fame. Suddenly she decides to become an actress. In the emotional confusion and frustration that comes by seeking to learn a new field she destroys the very principles and practices that brought her success.

A friend of mine is an electronics expert, a genius in the laboratory, an outstanding creator. Opportunity came along for him to organize his own company so he took his life savings and established a stock company in the very field in which he was successful. But he failed. He was unfamiliar with management. He did not know accounting. He did not know buying and selling, and he became so frustrated that he actually contemplated suicide. He was out of his depth, and his mind, in the principles that had led him to achieve. He went bankrupt. Now he is back in engineering and creating, where he belongs, but the experience has marked him for life.

Purpose and Uncontrolled Ambition

Remember the terrible story told by Albert Camus of a young man who had been gone from home for twenty-five years. He married, became wealthy and decided to return to the home of his childhood to visit his mother and sister. He arrived unannounced at the little inn his mother and sister operated. They did not recognize him so just for a joke he carried them on and did not reveal who he was. When he retired for the evening he was still pretending that he was just another traveler. That night his mother and sister robbed and killed him and threw his body into the river. They had been murdering travelers for years. To them he was no different from anyone else. When his wife, searching for him, came to the inn and told them her story they, from the shock of what they had done, killed themselves.

Can you find a more graphic illustration of the tragic luring that uncontrolled ambition brings? The only ones I can think of that are even more graphic are Hitler and Stalin and the other communist masters.

It is better to be a nobody, so to speak, and live a life of mediocrity than to let the evil of uncontrolled ambition make you its slave.

Purpose is our tool for success. Purpose is our instrument. It is enslaved to our will as the servant to the master but, oh, what a wonderful slave and servant controlled purpose is. Your key for success today is to learn to control your purpose. Make it a tremendous helper.

3. FINDING THE POWER OF PURPOSE

YOUR KEY for personal success is to find the power of purpose. What is the difference in one man and another? Here's a man who is dynamically, enthusiastically, vibrantly alive. Everything he does is charged with power. Here's another who droops, drags, and meanders through a mere existence. That difference is purpose. There is amazing power in purpose.

Do you realize that nearly 80 per cent of all high school and college students do not know what they are going to do? They are like the horses used during the threshing season on the farm. They go around and around and around every day, eating, sleeping and then back to the same old grind; or like the elevator operator, spending as much time going down as he is going up and never getting anywhere.

But you can't keep a purposeful man down. Take Clarence E. Birdseye for example. In 1924 he lost all of his money—everything he had, even the money borrowed on his life insurance—when his frozen food business failed. However he believed there was a market in frozen foods. He started over with $7.00 and borrowed a corner of a friend's ice plant for his experiments. Then five years later he sold out his frozen food company for $22,000,-000. Retire? Not Birdseye. He went on to secure more than two-hundred-fifty United States and foreign patents. In 1945 he came out with still another tremendous discovery in the food processing field.

H V. Kaltenborn quit high school after one year, moved from one job to another—lumber camp, war correspondent, door-to-door salesman—then went to school at Harvard, with only one year of high school, and graduated cum laude. He was the best known voice of broadcasting in America during World War II. He was a man with a powerful purpose.

One of the greatest achievements of purpose as well as one of the greatest joys is recognition. "Those who live nobly, even if in their life they live obscurely, need not fear that they will have lived in vain. Something radiates from their lives, some light that shows the way to their friends, their neighbors, perhaps to long future ages. I find many men nowadays oppressed with a sense of impotence, with a feeling that in the fastness of modern society there is nothing of importance that the individual can do." —Bertrand Russell.

Margaret Culkin Banning relates an interesting discussion. One man said to another that the lifetime savings of a certain friend had been swept away. A lady who overheard it said, "You mean that he lost his money." "Yes," the friend replied, "that's what I said." "No," said the lady, "you didn't say that. You told us that the savings of his lifetime were gone, which is not true. They're not gone. He has a mind stored full of knowledge and experience. He has made large investments in charity which haven't depreciated in yielding a return to society today. He saved his simple habits in his pleasure in living. You don't have to worry about him. He lives on."[1]

The man with a dynamic purpose doesn't jump out of a hotel window when depression comes. He realizes that the loss of money is simply a temporary detour on the road to success. When the crash in 1929 came a friend of mine went to his wife and said, "Well, honey, today we lost $160,000." Imagine the shock many women would have had if they had lost all that they possessed. However she was a woman of high purpose and deep spiritual insight. She smiled at her husband and said, "But, sweetheart, it is only money." That's the last thing they ever said about it.

Sir Thomas Buxton has said, "The longer I live the more I'm certain that the great difference between men, between the feeble and the powerful, between the great and the insignificant, is energy, *invincible determination of purpose once fixed and then death or victory*. This quality will do anything that can be done in this world; and without it no circumstances, no talents, no opportunities will make a two-legged creature a man."

Purpose Finds a Success Formula

"The important thing is not where you were or where you are but where you want to get," states Dr. Schwartz.[2] He suggests that you write out an image of yourself ten years from now:

    A. The Work Department ten years from now:
       1. What income level do I want to attain?
       2. What level of responsibility do I seek?

---

[1]Margaret Culkin Banning, *Indestructible Wealth*. Quoted by Earl Nightingale, *Our Changing World* No. 734 (Chicago: Nightingale-Conant Corporation).
[2]David J. Schwartz, *The Magic of Thinking Big* (Englewood Cliffs, N.J.: Prentice-Hall, Inc., 1959), pages 188-189.

3. How much authority do I want to command?
4. What prestige do I expect to gain from my work?

B. The Home Department ten years from now:
   1. What kind of standard of living do I want to provide for my family and myself?
   2. What kind of house do I want to live in?
   3. What kinds of vacations do I want to take?
   4. What financial support do I want to give my children in their early adult years?

C. Social Department ten years from now:
   1. What kind of friends do I want to have?
   2. What social groups do I want to join?
   3. What community leadership positions would I like to hold?
   4. What worthwhile causes do I want to champion?

There is power in such purpose as this.

If you really want something and want it bad enough and bring the intensity of all of your mind, your soul, your heart, your being to bear upon it you will achieve it. How many people will take something as it comes floating by but haven't the vision or the courage to make their utopia by applying the power of purpose that does achieve!

Dr. William C. Menninger, the world famous psychiatrist from Topeka, Kansas, in an article in *This Week Magazine* said: "Do you know whether you are going in the right direction and most of all where you want to go? Not just in your business alone but in the important personal areas: the atmosphere in your home, your relations with the members of your family, your own feeling of status and worthwhileness in life, your own dignity and your own integrity."[3] Check up on yourself. How do you measure up?

Have you ever had the fuel line in your automobile freeze up in the winter? Sometimes water will get in the gas tank and then freeze in the fuel line. It is impossible to start a car without gas. I remember one cold night when the temperature was in the teens having a friend push me for several miles through the crowded streets of St. Louis, not knowing that my fuel line was frozen. I finally had to

---

[3]Quoted by Earl Nightingale, *Our Changing World*, No. 930.

leave the car and come back the next day. When the weather had risen to a warmer temperature the gasoline flowed.

Earl Nightingale says that there are four reasons why people fail. In other words, there are four frozen points in the fuel line that keep the power of the fuel from getting to the motor of achievement. They are:

"(1) We don't have to.

"(2) We are doing about as well as the next guy.

"(3) We are using averages as standards to satisfactory performance.

"(4) We don't know we have so much reserve power and ability. We take ourselves for granted."[4]

Put the heat of excitement, enthusiasm to your frozen power lines. You can be successful.

The person who dares to dedicate himself to high and lofty purpose will have power. The power is there. It is inborn. We always have the energy to do the things that we enjoy doing. Have you ever seen a teenage boy come in from school, from football practice or from exercise and flop down on the couch and claim he was too tired to study? No energy, exhausted, worn out, but let his girl friend drive by and toot the horn. He bounds off the couch, runs through the house, leaving the front door ajar, and rushes out to the car, not taking the time to recall that he's exhausted. He comes back after an hour's drive exhilarated. You see he had energy for doing what he wanted to do.

So like the husband who has no energy on his day off to finish mowing the grass, or to paint the shutter, or to haul out the garbage, but has plenty of energy to go fishing, or to play golf. The power comes with the intensity of purpose.

No Purpose in the Home

One of the problems of family life in America today is the tragedy of men with no purpose, men who simply, under the pressures of finance or the home or whatever, walked away and left the wife and children to struggle for themselves. Many, many times have I had to assist in such circumstances. You see these men were trying to escape from life's responsibilities. They had no purpose. Howev-

---

[4]*Our Changing World*, No. 811.

er, the power to provide for a family is there for a purposeful man.

In one of his radio addresses Earl Nightingale gives three things to do to become rich[5]:

(1) Make up your mind that there is no good reason why you can't get the money you and your family want. If other people can get rich so can you. The largest industrial empires in this country were started by the idea of a single individual and they all started as small businesses.

(2) Decide on the exact amount you want to earn and set a time limit for yourself. Be realistic and sensible. Ask yourself what your qualifications are and set up a reasonable amount in a reasonable length of time. At the same time make up your mind that you are going to concentrate on this exclusively until you reach your goal.

(3) The magic formula for financial success has never changed since the first coins were minted in Asia Minor. It is six words: "Find a need and fill it." That's your part of the bargain. Don't go afield into areas in which you have no experience. Is it easy? No, but it works. The power is available for a man who has high purpose.

The Cleveland, Ohio, manufacturing firm of Warner and Swasey recently in an ad said, "It wasn't the Goths that defeated Rome. It was the free circuses. . . . Luxuries, power, indulgence had made the once tough Roman people soft. To stay popular their Emperors gave them more and more of the ease they craved—free bread, free circuses, easy living, so the Romans softened up themselves for the ambitious, hard-working barbarians and in A.D. 410 the greatest nation the world had ever seen was invaded and destroyed." Half of all the people in the then known world were slaves, working for the other half. The majority of the people living in Rome were on relief. The government had become their benefactor. Their will to live was destroyed. They had lost their purpose. And never forget it could happen in America today.

A ten-year study of men in various occupations conducted by General Motors Research Institute showed that as men advanced in their responsibilities and positions their mental and emotional capacity increased markedly as well as their ability to withstand strain. In other words men with high purpose not only live longer they have the power to produce more!

---

[5] *Our Changing World*, No. 769.

How purpose can help you make a habit of succeeding:

1. Write out below the most important objective you could achieve in your lifetime.

2. State the benefits of this life-long achievement:

    A. To family

    B. To business or professional associates

    C. Religious and social

    D. National

3. Are you willing to alter the pattern of your life to achieve this purpose?

4. State how you will alter your life.

William James said, "The greatest discovery of my generation is that human beings can alter their lives by altering their attitudes of mind."

4. DEVELOPING PURPOSE

YOUR KEY to personal success is to build a dynamic purpose. How do we develop purpose?

According to Charles B. Roth there are seven motives of life:

(1) Health. Everyone wants it and seeks it.

(2) Wealth. (Some think the most dominant drive in many people's lives.)

(3) Gratification of appetite—hunger and thirst for physical things but for mental and emotional as well.

(4) Amusement—entertainment, games, recreation, all forms of diversion.

(5) Security. This is important.

(6) Vanity—the desire to be admired. This motive is always important in influencing others.

(7) Self-improvement.[1]

Study these motives. You will find that they will help develop dynamic purpose in your life.

Making money will not necessarily make you happy. You must have a stronger, greater goal than that of just financial security. Jesus of Nazareth established a new standard when He gave us the rule that service is greatness.

A Cause Greater Than Self

Remember the Biblical truth that he who would exalt himself shall be humble and he who humbles himself shall be exalted. This paradox is surprising to some. Have you ever noticed the persons who exalted themselves, living only for the purpose of satisfying their own desires—the Hitlers, the Mussolinis, the Napoleons, the Capones? Lincoln and Ghandi stand in sharp contrast. When a person dedicates his life and time and effort and energy to a cause greater than himself he develops a dynamic purpose that truly makes life a romance and glorious adventure. One of my mottoes is, "The greatest use of life is to so live your life that the use of your life will outlive your life." Finding this cause is the first step in developing purpose. Now you are really beginning to live.

Dr. Chester A. Swor said, "An opportunity grasped and used produces at least one other opportunity."

Let's say that your motto or your purpose, your goal, your objective is to make other people happy. Now look at its long-range aspect. It will affect your insurance program. You will not be selfish enough to spend your entire income on yourself. You will provide for the possi-

---

[1]Charles B. Roth, *Winning Personal Recognition* (Englewood Cliffs, N.J.: Prentice-Hall, Inc., 1954), pages 30-31.

bility of your death by meeting the needs of others through an adequate insurance program. You will establish a long-range effectiveness by saving. Every week lay aside something for the inevitable rainy day. This will affect you in your personal health, pay off in the enrichment of your life. Expanding your life over a longer period of time will enable you to make others happy longer.

But also look at the short-range aspect of it. Everything you do will seek to lift those others round about you. Remember those lines, "When I met him I was looking down; when I left him I was looking up." The taxi driver, the bus driver, the doorman, the elevator operator, the clerk in the store, the waitress at lunch, the secretary at the office, the client, the customer—nearly everyone else has more problems than you have. Why don't you set your purpose to making other people happy?

Commit Yourself

To develop an effective purpose it must be written out. It must be stamped indelibly upon your mind by repetition. Write it out and put it over the dashboard of your car, above the mirror in the morning, over the sink and certainly in your billfold. Never forget that we develop a purpose by making it become a steadfast habit of our life.

Your Seeking Mind

The next step in developing your purpose is to make real in your life the words of Aristotle when he said, "All men desire by nature to know." Yes, we have some people in America who have been educated beyond their intelligence. But they are the rare exception. Isn't the ceaseless desire for knowledge one of the most outstanding contributions that an education can give a person? Remember that old story of a boy who was on his way home from college and had all of his college notes for four years catalogued very carefully in his trunk but in a train wreck the trunk was destroyed by the ensuing fire. He was not injured but he had to go back for four more years to gain more notes.

Equally tragic is the person who files away in his Fibber

McGee closet all of the information and inspiration that he had in college, never to desire further knowledge.

Recall the times you have gone into your favorite drug store and asked the druggist for a particular item. He knew immediately where it was. He also knew about further developments in that field. For example there may be a competitive product that has recently come out that is better than the one you are accustomed to, and he may make this observation and suggest its use to you. Here is a man who has knowledge of the product and a knowledge of his store. But most important of all he knows you and your needs. That's why you keep going back. Here is a man who is successful. He is persistently increasing his knowledge in order to serve you better.

Make No Little Plans

For the further development of your purpose you must make big plans. For many years I have been quoting Daniel Burnham of the Chicago Plan Commission. I believe Mr. Burnham was the first man to develop one of America's shopping centers. The whole structure of our city and urban life has been changed by this man's vision. Remember his words, "Make no little plans. There is nothing in little plans to stir men's blood. Make big plans. Once a big idea is recorded it can never die."

You have never known a little man to come up with a big idea. This is true in this life and in the next, for Jesus said: "Thou hast been faithful over a few things, I will make thee the ruler over many things."

No janitor ever immediately became president but some of America's industrial giants began as janitors. In the process they were painstakingly successful in accomplishing the first plan, then they raised their goal—their purpose, vision, aspirations, intentions—to another and then another and on until they achieved the pinnacle of their goal of success. How big are your plans? How long has it been since you analyzed them? Are they big enough to stir your blood and other men's blood as well?

Earl Nightingale has discussed some of the things people want to gain in life, what they want to be and what they want to save.[2]

They want to gain: (1) Health. (2) Time. (3) Money.

---

[2] *Our Changing World,* Nos. 720, 820.

(4) Popularity. (5) Improved appearance. (6) Security in old age. (7) Praise from others. (8) Comfort. (9) Leisure. (10) Pride of accomplishment. (11) Advancement, business and social. (12) Increased enjoyment. (13) Self-confidence. (14) Personal prestige.

What people want to be: (1) Good parents. (2) Sociable. (3) Up to date. (4) Creative. (5) Proud of their possessions. (6) Influential over others. (7) Gregarious. (8) Efficient. (9) First in things. (10) Recognized as authority.

What people want to save: (1) Time. (2) Money. (3) Work. (4) Discomfort. (5) Worry. (6) Doubts. (7) Risk. (8) Personal embarrassment. But none of these things can be yours without first developing a dynamic purpose.

Let me suggest that you get the book *TNT, The Power Within You* by Claude M. Bristol and Harold Sherman and by all means major on the chapter "How to Build Mind Pictures." There is an ancient saying, "Look within. Within is the fountain of good and let it bubble up if thou would ever dig." Now as you think in mind pictures, picture yourself as you want to be, accomplishing the things you desire, achieving the goals you have set for yourself. You will find that this is the most magnetized picture you have ever imagined. You will draw the strength, knowledge and power to accomplish it because you have established it as a visual picture.

This picture will become the pattern of your success. It will be mental television. You will see yourself accomplishing all that you desire. Never forget the words from the Bible in Mark 11:24: "Therefore I say unto you, What things soever ye desire, when ye pray, believe that ye receive them and ye shall have them." The minute you establish this dynamic purpose and begin the persistent achievement of this challenging, worthy goal you become successful that very moment; for so often the achieving, the accomplishing, the realizing, the journey itself means far more than the privilege of having arrived.

This then will be your success insurance. You will be a dynamic, dedicated man whom nothing can stop. And never forget that those who are following you will take strength, inspiration and challenge from you—your children, your associates, your employees and employers and all of your social, church and community friends.

5. PURPOSE GROUNDED IN ACHIEVEMENT

YOUR KEY for personal success is dynamic, invigorating purpose.

For purpose to be all consuming, powerful and challenging it must be grounded in success and achievement in little endeavors. Persistent achievement brings the challenge for greater purpose. Achievement comes from seeing and recognizing a need, and from purposeful action resulting in the solution of that need.

A need is a gap between a stimulus aroused and that stimulus achieved. This achievement comes when the task is completed and well done. The vast majority of us have the joy of achievement in the present. Johann Sebastian Bach had been dead twenty-five years before the musical public was willing to accept his compositions. It was still another quarter of a century before his true greatness was acknowledged around the world. He was buried in a pauper's field; but today he is accepted as one of the most outstanding musicians the world has ever known. Here's the tragedy of achievement coming too late. However, this need not be so in your life. You can know the joy of achievement as a result of your purpose now.

Don't Sell Yourself Short

"I'm a practicing psychologist," said Randall B. Hamrack.[1] "In twenty years I've talked with, tested and given vocational counsel to at least 10,000 young men and women. One characteristic that almost all had was the tendency to sell themselves short. We need not worry about the bright educated. His kind is not very common. But we do need to worry about the legions of young people who underestimate themselves. When at least three out of four sell themselves short we are suffering a community tragedy that is compounded by the individual trag-

---

[1]Quoted in *Our Changing World*, No. 633.

edy of each unfulfilled life." Did you catch the scope of that? Three-fourths of all the young people in America sell themselves short; they are not measuring up to their total personality, therefore they are living mediocre, meaningless existences. America can't reach her heights unless our young people are dynamically motivated to purposeful action.

You're Responsible for Your Face

The story is told that one of Lincoln's advisors urgently recommended a candidate for appointment to Lincoln's cabinet and Lincoln declined to follow his suggestion. So he was asked to give his reason. "I don't like the man's face," Lincoln explained. "But the poor man is not responsible for his face," insisted his supporter. "Every man over forty is responsible for his face," Lincoln replied, and turned away to resume discussion of other matters.

I believe Lincoln was right. Medical scientists tell us that the will to live is one of the most important, if not the most important factor in a sick person's getting well. I have talked with patients who had decided to die. I've seen some take my challenge and as they responded dynamically and enthusiastically their medical case history immediately reversed itself.

If this is true with a sick person how much more true is it with a well person. Therefore your purpose actually will affect your looks. A person with dynamic purpose is a person who is on fire—a person living for new goals, a person living for the fullest in life. The excitement and vigorous life will show on his face.

Life Purpose

Let me suggest three purposes of your life and, if you will practice them, I can assure you that you will enjoy the true results of dynamic purpose.

1. One is service. Jesus taught us to serve. Rome had ruled the minds and will of others with its might. To the Romans, "might was right." You and I know that he who would be great must be the greatest servant. You can have a dynamic life but it is necessary that you seize every opportunity to serve.

Would you like to know God's will for your life in service? The following will help you find it: (A) Do you see a needed task? Maybe it's a Boy Scout troop that needs a leader. Maybe it's the establishment of a Boy's Club. Maybe it's a P.T.A. responsibility, or a Sunday school class. Maybe it's an invalid who needs a visit or a person in jail who needs a friend. Maybe it's a family that needs food. See the opportunity. (B) Say to yourself, "By the grace of God I can do that." (C) Start doing it. Get right at it. (D) If God doesn't stop you, that's His plan for your life.

"The secret of success in life is for a man to be ready for his opportunity when it comes."—Benjamin Disraeli.

Remember that serving takes effort. "When God wanted sponges and oysters He made them and put one on a rock and the other in the mud. When He made man he did not make him to be a sponge or an oyster; He made him with feet and hands, and head and heart, and vital blood, and a place to use them and He said to him, 'Go work.'" —Henry Ward Beecher.

2. Leadership that you give to others is a true result of purpose. Everyone is looking for someone to say, "Well done." How well I remember my high school and college days when my coaches in athletic events would say a word of commendation after a particularly hard effort, whether in practice or in the game. In high school I would have done anything for Joe Robert Gouldman's words of appreciation. I wanted above everything else, seemingly, to satisfy my coach. The same was true of Stanley Robinson in college. This is the power of purposeful leadership.

Never forget you are the leader someone is looking to. Every boy wants to be like his dad. Every girl wants to be like her mother. One of the greatest things a man can do is to leave a purposeful heritage, to leave an example of dynamic purposeful leadership.

When Lee Scarborough returned from Harvard Law School and Baylor University to his West Texas town the crowds came to hear him preach his first sermon. Some of the men who heard it were weighing the difference between his country preacher father, limited in education, and the well-trained son. One said, "Well, he can out-preach his dad." They were shocked when the man in front of them turned, and they recognized Lee's father. He sparkled with their words, smiled broadly and said, "That's the finest compliment you could give me, for you see he's standing on my shoulders." That is that result of purpose, a leadership that others seek to follow.

3. A third result of purpose is impact. What you do for good, what you do in purposeful success will be a part of the total triumph of democracy. Andrew Carnegie has so well said, "No man can become rich himself without in turn enriching others." If you come to the end of life's journey and can honestly look back and see in the trail of your years many people wonderfully blessed, lifted up from their discouragement because you passed their way, people whose livelihood, happiness, achievement were accomplished as a result of your encouragement, then you have made a definite contribution to the way of life that we believe is the best ever known or achieved on the face of this planet.

As Dale Carnegie so well said, "Instead of worrying about what people say of you why not spend your time trying to accomplish something they will admire." And do it honestly.

Don't forget those words from Jeremiah 17:11: "As the partridge sitteth on eggs, and hatcheth them not; so he that getteth riches, and not by right, shall leave them in the midst of his days, and at his end shall be a fool." Honesty—strict and uncompromising—is still the best way to run a business or to get wealthy in this world.

Back before the turn of the century a Christian business merchant in Philadelphia by the name of John Wanamaker decided that his convictions demanded that he practice the golden rule in business. He sought to satisfy the customer. He was laughed at. People said it would never work. Do you know what happened? Today his desire to satisfy the customer is one of the prevailing principles of business in America. "The customer is always right." There isn't room to list all the large, successful business firms in America built upon this principle.

Yes, Wanamaker made a contribution, a lasting, effective, dynamic contribution to all that western men believe in. He was a part of the total triumph of democracy and of righteousness.

How to Develop Purpose

The habit of a developed purpose equals success:

1. Restate your life-long purpose.

2. Is this purpose a cause greater than yourself?

    A. Are other people happier?

    B. Are all others enriched?

3. What habit of personal improvement have you developed?

    A. Dale Carnegie Leadership Course?

    B. Dale Carnegie Sales Course?

    C. The Science of Personal Achievement Course?

    D. A Professional Course?

    E. Others?

4. List the twelve things people want in life in order of importance according to you:

    A.
    B.
    C.
    D.
    E.
    F.
    G.
    H.
    I.

J.
K.
L.

5. Are you producing greater service?

6. Are you producing greater leadership?

7. Is our nation stronger for having experienced you?

8. Is the torch of your purpose worth handing on to the succeeding generations?

PART TWO
GOALS CAN CHANGE YOUR LIFE

6. ESTABLISHING A GOAL

YOUR KEY for personal success is to establish a goal. Goals and purpose are different. Purpose is the long range—the pot of gold at the end of the rainbow. When you reach out for it it is still ahead of you. Goals may be long range but they are more clearly defined.

What Goals Are

Notice three things about goals.

1. Goals are concrete. They are concrete actions we can and intend to do.

2. Goals are measurable. They afford measures so we can judge our progress. They may be quantitative—how much we intend to do and how often. They may be in terms of time—how soon we plan to accomplish them.

3. Goals are related to a definite period. They are definite time targets—an intent to accomplish a result for that particular period. While objectives may be pursued for indefinite times in the future, goals are what we determine to do within our planning period to move toward the objective.

The Dynamics of Setting Goals

Frank Bettger, one of America's outstanding salesmen and lecturer on sales and author of three popular books for salesmen, spends Friday afternoon setting up next week's work. Frank even schedules his haircut. On the weekend he developed an intensity of purpose, a dynamic desire. He went to work on Monday morning vibrantly alive. You see, there are dynamics in setting goals.

Know Where You're Going

Thomas A. Edison said, "The most important factors of invention can be described in a few words. They consist first of definite knowledge as to what one wishes to achieve. One must fix his mind on that purpose with persistence and begin searching for that which he seeks, making use of all of the accumulated knowledge of the subject which he has or can acquire from others. He must keep on searching no matter how many times he may meet with disappointment. He must refuse to be influenced by the fact that somebody else may have tried the same idea without success. He must keep himself sold on the idea that the solution of his problem exists somewhere and that he will find it. . . .

"When a man makes up his mind to solve any problem he may at first meet with dogged opposition, but if he holds on and keeps on searching he will be sure to find some sort of solution. The trouble with most people is that they quit before they start."

Dr. Alexander Graham Bell said, "I had made up my mind to find that for which I was searching even if it required the remainder of my life. After innumerable failures I finally uncovered the principle for which I was searching, and I was astounded at its simplicity. I was still more astounded to discover the principle I had revealed was not only beneficial in the construction of a mechanical hearing aid but it served as well as a means of sending the sound of the voice over a wire. Another discovery which came out of my investigation was the fact that when a man gives his order to produce a definite result and stands by that order it seems to have the effect of giving him what might be termed a second sight which enables him to see right through ordinary problems. What this power is I cannot say; all I know is that it exists and it becomes available only when a man is in that state of mind in which he knows exactly what he wants and is fully determined not to quit until he finds it."

Team Power

An excellent example of the dynamics of setting goals is the intensity of purpose, the strength of discipline that's involved in an athletic team, particularly a high school group. The hardest work I ever did in my life was getting in shape for football, both in high school and college. While tearing around the field at the end of practice as darkness was spreading across the stadium I used to say to myself, "This is the hardest work you have ever done. Why do you continue to do it?" Why? I did it to make the team. I did it to help win the game. I did it for the recognition of the school. I did it for my teammates. The goal was there and the dynamics resulted.

Have you ever thought about the dynamics of riding a bicycle? You have to get up a certain amount of speed before you can hold the bicycle on course. A man is like riding a bicycle. When we have the dynamics of a goal it develops the equilibrium necessary to move the bicycle forward. But when we slow down, the bicycle wobbles and will finally fall.

Dr. Maxwell Maltz in his book *Psycho-cybernetics* says: "We are engineered as goal-seeking mechanisms. We are built that way. When we have no personal goal which we are interested in and means something in us, we have to go around in circles, feel lost and find life itself aimless and purposeless. We are built to conquer environment, solve problems, achieve goals and we find no real satisfaction or happiness in life without obstacles to conquer and goals to achieve. People who say that life is not worthwhile are really saying that they themselves have no personal goals which are worthwhile. Get yourself a goal worth working for. Better still, get yourself a project. Decide what you want out of a situation. Always have something ahead to look forward to."[1]

Find out what you really want to do in life above everything else. Determine your goal. Visualize it in your mind. Picture what you want to be, the kind of person you want to become.

Then get all the facts about it. Get everything that is possible from the public library, from your personal rating and experience of others, from every bit of information you can gather. Analyze, discuss and test these facts. Put them in logical order. Determine how you are going to accomplish your goal.

The next thing to do is to set a time schedule. Don't let anything divert you to chasing rabbits. Stay on the path. Finally don't just talk about it, get at it. Start out this very moment. Remember that a journey of a thousand miles begins with one step. So start in. You can be successful.

A little goal soon reaches its realization. The same intensity of effort brought to bear upon a large goal will

---

[1]Maxwell Maltz, *Psycho-cybernetics* (Englewood Cliffs, N.J.: Prentice-Hall, Inc., 1960), pages 57-58.

inevitably result in the same accomplishment. If your wife wants a new dress or a new hat, she will find a way to get it—out of the grocery money, out of savings, put it on the bill—somehow she will get it. Plato said, "A work well begun is half ended." And of course the best way to begin a work is to have faith that inevitably it will be successfully completed. Remember the words of Paul J. Meyer, "What you ardently desire, sincerely believe in, vividly imagine, enthusiastically act on must inevitably come to pass."

Energy Unlimited

Often people ask me, "Where do you get your energy?" Arnold Bennett has given us the best answer to this question: "Perhaps you've been hoping to create energy in yourself. Now you cannot create energy in yourself or elsewhere. Nobody can. You can only set energy free, loosen it, transform it, direct it. An individual is born with a certain amount of energy, no more. And what is more important you cannot put additional qualities into it. You may sometimes seem to be putting energy into him but you are not; you are simply setting this original energy free—applying a match to the coal or fanning the fire. Some people seem to lack energy when as a fact they are full of energy which is merely dormant, waiting for the match or waiting for direction. The usual idea of the amount of energy possessed by an individual is the intensity of the desire of that person. It is desire that uses energy. Strong desires generally betoken much energy—and they are definite desires. Without desire energy is rendered futile. Nobody will consume energy in action unless he desires to perform the action, either for itself or as a means to a desired end.

"You must not confuse vague, general aspiration with desire. A real desire is definite, concrete. The desire which indicates great energy is always there, worrying. It is an obsession—a whip, it has no mercy."

I have goals in life. I have purposes to perform; I've written out these purposes and they make my life wonderfully and joyfully worth living. You see, goals set our innate energies free.

The greatest dynamics come during the setting of the goal and the process of reaching it. Once the goal is reached there is a natural letdown. Far too many people rest on their oars and drift into some secluded cove never to establish another goal. They literally deteriorate with inactivity. Some people die at thirty and are buried at seventy. In fact, I know some who have been embalmed but haven't been laid away yet! So is the one who has reached a goal but stops there. Goals are temporary rest points on the journey to a fulness in life. We pause to reflect—to look back and examine. We pause to get our breath and energy and to set our direction for the next height to scale. The climb itself is far more invigorating, stimulating and dynamically enthusiastic than reaching the height itself.

This truth is so well described in the words of a philosopher who said, "There is not much to do but bury a man when the last of his dreams is dead." Henry J. Kaiser turned over his huge business interest to his son and went to Hawaii to retire. But a man with dynamic goals can't rest and can't retire. So he set out to build first one hotel, then others, then a beautiful office building with a revolving restaurant on top. Today Waikiki is a fabulous development, all because of the dream and the goals of one man. As Earl Nightingale has said, "A person is as young as his dreams—or as old as his doubts." Let each goal be a temporary pause on the road to greater achievement.

7. THE DISCIPLINE OF GOALS

YOUR KEY for personal success for today is the discipline of goals. Every person should read Napoleon Hill's *Think and Grow Rich*. In it he has listed ten causes for failure in leadership. They are: "(1) Inability to organize details. (2) Unwillingness to render humble service. (3) Expectation of pay for what they know instead of what they do with that which they know. (4) Fear of competition from followers. (5) Lack of imagination. (6) Selfishness. (7) Intemperance. (8) Disloyalty. (9) Emphasis of the authority of leadership. (10) Emphasis of title."[1]

Each of these qualities of failure is the result of a lack of goals. For goals intensely established, regularly checked on, ardently desired, bring wonderful discipline of action.

Harry Emerson Fosdick once wrote, "No horse gets anywhere till he's harnessed, no steam or gas drives anything until it's confined, no Niagara ever turned anything into light or power until it's tunneled, no life ever grows great until focused, dedicated and disciplined."

Ninety-five Per Cent Fail

Take a hundred men at age twenty-five all expecting to be successful. If you will trace these men through forty years of business life, you will find, as they face retirement, one is rich, four are independently wealthy, five are still working, thirty-six have died and fifty-four are dead broke. Now if each one of those men would only save 10 per cent of what he makes and if he never made more than $6,000 a year he would have set aside $24,000 during that forty years of business experience. Now at normal interest rates this $24,000 would have grown to $58,000. Certainly that's an adequate figure to keep the wolf away from the door. But why is it that so many men don't do it? They simply have no goal. They have no purpose. They do not have the discipline of a purpose out ahead. They do not write down their goal and bring all their energy to bear upon it.

Alexander Maclaren said, "The man who has not learned to say no will be a weak if not a wretched man as long as he lives." He will have no goals, no discipline, no joy, no achievement, no provision for family, no nest egg for a rainy day, no investment for that opportunity of financial growth.

The Apostle Paul became the greatest follower of his Master the world has ever known by the impact of his life and by the dedication of his efforts. You see he had a goal. It is recorded in Philippians 3:13: "This one thing I do, forgetting those things which are behind, and reaching

[1]Napoleon Hill, *Think and Grow Rich*, rev. ed. (Chicago: Combined Registry Company, 1960), pages 107-109.

forth unto those things which are before, I press toward the mark."

Would you go hunting a Rocky Mountain bear with a shotgun full of bird shot? No. The bird shot is so diffused by the shotgun that even if it hits the target, which is possible but unlikely, it will not accomplish the purpose of killing the game. No, you take a high-powered rifle for big game—one that will reach the goal and can kill when it reaches. This is the secret of a goal. Instead of scattering our efforts in diffused activity a goal brings the single-mindedness of purpose.

A One-Eyed Man

Be a one-eyed man. That's what Jesus was saying when he said, "When thine eye is single, thy whole body also is full of light." Be then a one-eyed man. That's what Andrew Carnegie was when he said, "Put all your eggs in one basket and watch that basket." Concentrate on one purpose and then you will be successful.

"A shockingly large number of our worries and our hidden tensions stem from the fact that millions of people have never found themselves, and never discovered the kind of work they could love and do well. Instead they seeth with inner rebellion because they spend their lives doing work they despise." —Dale Carnegie.

Can you find a better definition of the diffused life with no purpose, no plan, no goal?

"The educated man is the man who has learned how to get every thing he needs without violating the rights of his fellow men. Education comes from within; you get it by struggle and effort and thought."—Napoleon Hill.

Your key for personal success is to establish a definite goal, for in the dynamics of its purpose there will be the discipline that will lead you to personal success. Remember that the definition of success is the persistent achievement of a challenging, worthy goal. I dare you to be different. I dare you to be personally, dynamically successful. You can be. Establish your goal and you will. It is inevitable. You will!

8. EXAMPLES OF GOALS

YOUR KEY for personal success is goals. In this section there are examples of goals that have made men's lives dynamic. Sallust said, "Every man is the architect of his own fortune." Do you believe that?

A Formula for Goal Success

Framed in my office is the motto of another dynamic individual who owes his success to the setting of goals. His is called the million dollar personal success plan. Paul J. Meyer was a millionaire at twenty-six. Here is his formula:

"(1) Crystallize your thinking. Determine what specific goal you want to achieve. Then dedicate yourself to its attainment with unswerving singleness of purpose, the trenchant zeal of a crusader.

"(2) Develop a plan for achieving your goal and a deadline for its attainment. Plan your projects carefully—hour by hour, day by day, month by month. Organize activity and maintain enthusiasm of the well springs of your power.

"(3) Develop a sincere desire for the things you want in life. A burning desire is the greatest motivator of every human action. The desire for success implants success consciousness which in turn creates a vigorous and ever-increasing habit of success.

"(4) Develop supreme confidence in yourself and your own abilities. Enter every activity without giving mental recognition to the possibility of defeat. Concentrate on your strengths instead of your weaknesses; on your powers instead of your problems.

"(5) Develop a dogged determination to follow through on your plan regardless of obstacles, criticisms or circumstances. Construct your determination with sustained effort—controlled attention and concentrated energy. Opportunities never come to those who wait—they are captured by those who dare to attack."[1]

Paul Meyer left his native California and headed for the Eastern Seaboard expecting to learn life insurance. His first stop was in Columbus, Georgia, where he nearly starved to death for the first six months because some agent simply threw a rate book at him and said, "Here, poor sucker, root hog or die." But in that six-month period he learned some principles of life insurance. By the time he was twenty-three he was vice-president of the insurance company and had the largest volume of business for any man his age in America. He was called upon to be the speaker at the Million Dollar Round Table. Today he is the president of Success Motivation Institute of Waco, Texas, a living, dynamic example that goals do pay off.

Two Hundred Success Stories

In the book *You Are Better Than You Think* by Albert, Dr. Charlotte Buhler of the Psychological Institute in Vienna reports the study of lives of 200 famous men and women. They discovered that in every case there was a self-selected goal that directed all the energies of the individual.[2] "Write down what you want to achieve. Then frame the paper on which you have written it and hang it on the wall," said Johnson O'Conner.

Lawrence Gould, the psychologist commented, "Many a man has been puzzled at the lack of results from his grim determination to succeed when his real unconscious desire was to have a good time and to take life easy—a picture that often comes in my mind is the scene in the old-fashioned melodrama when the heroine pretends to yield to the villain's embraces, but behind her back waves a white handkerchief to call the hero to the rescue."

To achieve any goal there must be the conscious and the unconscious commitment of all that you are to the dedication of the effort of that goal. There must be harmony. There must be energy. There must be oneness in purpose if you are to reach your goal. Dora Albert gives a simple plan for achieving your goals:

---

[1]Conversation with Paul J. Meyer.
[2]Dora Albert, *You Are Better Than You Think* (Englewood Cliffs, N.J.: Prentice-Hall, Inc., 1957), page 193.

"(1) Find out what your unconscious goal is by studying what you have accomplished so far.

"(2) Figure out where your conscious goal corresponds with what you do. For instance, if your goal is success and you are drinking your way to failure whom are you kidding?

"(3) Visualize yourself succesfully realizing and achieving your goal.

"(4) Write a summary to yourself, telling yourself exactly what specific steps are needed to achieve it. If you need additional educational training write down what kind of training. Then plan to get it.

"(5) Write a letter or make a phone call that will help you take the next step toward your goal.

"(6) Include recreation and fun in your goals. Plan some healthful recreational activity at least once each week.

"(7) Make sure that your goals are consistent with your self-esteem. If you have to kick someone else to achieve your goal you won't be happy reaching it.

"(8) Make sure that your goal represents something you want to do not just what you think you ought to do. Regardless of what your parents or friends think you ought to do examine your own heart and mind."[8] That is excellent advice. Listen to it. Follow the example of others and you too can be amazingly successful.

Five Per Cent Excell

In America today only one person out of every 1,220 taxpayers is a millionaire; one out of every 144 taxpayers earns from $25,000 to $50,000 a year; one family out of nineteen earns $10,000 a year—that's about 5 per cent. That means that 95 per cent of the people earn less than $10,000 a year. Now if you are negative you will say that the reason you aren't in that select one-of-nineteen group is because you lack education or because you were not at the right place at the right time, or you didn't have the right pull, or you didn't marry a woman with wealth, or some other excuse. Don't forget the words of Andrew Carnegie, "No man becomes rich unless he enriches others." That's how he made his $500,000,000. He did it by

---

[8]Albert, *Ibid.*, pages 195-198.

lowering the price of steel from $160 a ton to $20 a ton. He benefited all Americans.

Yes, the reason you are in the 95 per cent category if you are, is because you planned it that way. You did not set a goal. Let me question very seriously if you should set a goal for money alone. The goal should be to render a greater service than someone else. If you do this the money will come rolling in.

Emerson said, "If a man has good corn, or wood, or boards, or pigs to sell, or can make better chairs or knives, crucibles or church organs than anybody else you will find a broad, hard-beaten road to his house though it be in the woods."

Have you heard Charles M. Simmons' record, *The Magic Key?*[4] Simmons gives us some marvelous advice:

I. Ask yourself the question, "What do I want to accomplish today?" Most people never ask it. People who fail never plan. Remember nothing becomes dynamic until it first becomes specific.

II. Ask yourself, "How strong is my desire?"
   A. Do you get up early in the morning?
   B. Will you contact ten people today by phone or letter?
   C. Will you make an advance plan to be enthusiastic even if you don't feel like it?
   D. Why not carry a hundred dollar bill? It gives you money consciousness and a sense of success.
   E. Do you buy and wear good clothes? It pays. You see clothes cover 96 per cent to 98 per cent of the man. Clothes do make the man.
   F. Do you read good inspirational books? And of course the best inspirational book is the Bible.
   G. Go to church on Sunday with your family. Make it a family affair.
   H. Ask for that order. Go out expecting to give better service to your client than anybody else in this world.

III. Now ask yourself, "What is my deadline?" Set a timetable for reaching your long-range goals. Write

---

[4]You can secure it by writing 630 North San Mateo Drive, San Mateo, California. Another outstanding record is Earl Nightingale's *The Strangest Secret in the World.*

out a check to yourself for a certain amount at a
certain time. Then expect to cash it.

IV. Ask yourself, "What is my exact plan of action?"
And then, "How do I start?" "How do I go about
it?"

Such advice will make you a dynamic man. I challenge
you to try it.

Five Success Suggestions

Five suggestions for success are:

(1) Pay the price. Results are directly proportionate to
the effort we put forth. We must understand emotionally
that as we sow so do we reap.

(2) Can you practice imagination? Can you see yourself
achieving every bit of the goal you've attempted?

(3) Practice courage. Talk positively on your goal.
Refuse to believe that there is any circumstance sufficient
to its defeat.

(4) Save 10 per cent of what you earn. Make your
dollars your slaves to work for you.

(5) Action. The achievement of this program of success
demands immediate dynamic action. This then is the example of goals.

9. BENEFITS OF GOALS

YOUR KEY for personal success for today is found in the
benefits of goals. There are abilities in goals. You can be
successful.

French moralist, Jean de la Bruyère said, "In this world
there are only two ways of getting on—either by one's
own industry or by the imbecility of others." You may
"get on" the latter way, but you haven't been successful,
for success is the persistent achievement of a challenging
and worthy goal. The greatest benefit of a dynamic goal is
that you yourself measure up to the fullest possibility of

the total capacity of all of your talents, mind power and potential.

Goal Happiness

One of the outstanding benefits of goals is personal happiness. Life is too short to be unhappy. But you will never be happy until you are achieving a worthy challenging goal. And remember it cannot be selfish nor can it be evil. A worthy goal will benefit you. It will benefit your family. It will benefit your community. It will benefit your church. It will benefit your society, yea, even the nation. You see, your abilities are very closely related to your desires. If you desire little you will exercise little of your capacity. I will tell you who the outstanding athletes are. They are the ones who paid the greatest price, such as Leroy Jordan of Alabama football fame who in the fall of 1962 made All-American. Although smaller than many other college linemen, Leroy Jordan made up in determination, dedication, and desire what he lacked in weight and natural ability. He wanted to play college football and dedicated himself to this purpose rather than dissipating his abilities in a hundred inconsistent activities. I saw Leroy in the Orange Bowl January 1, 1963. There was an example of outstanding dedication to a goal. Remember that high school athlete you knew who had such natural ability? Where is he now? Lost in the swamp of mediocrity. He didn't have a goal. All of that ability was wasted. No purpose, no goal.

Remember when you were young you used to hear people say that rich people aren't happy. Only poor people are really happy. Do you believe this? Is this true? Marcus Antoninus remarked, "No man is happy who does not think himself so." A man may have riches and be miserable. That man is not a successful man. But the man who has set a dynamic goal is happy because he is persistently achieving that worthy, challenging goal. And this in itself brings about peace and happiness of mind. Augustine said, "Happiness comes in the attainment of our desires and in our having only right desires."

Failure Sours

"Men, on the average, will be kindly or hostile in their feelings toward each other in the proportion that they feel their lives unsuccessful or successful." —Bertrand Russell.

"The common idea that success spoils people by making them vain, egotistic and self complacent is erroneous; on the contrary it makes them for the most part humble, tolerant and kind. Failure makes people bitter and cruel." —W. Somerset Maugham.

A person may have a hundred million dollars and be a failure. And the widow who sets her goal to provide the best possible education for her child and to give him the best possible character training may die a pauper but leave an immortal influence. This truly is success—the persistent achievement of a worthy, challenging goal.

Goal Enthusiasm

As Dale Carnegie has so well put it, "If you want to be happy set yourself a goal that demands your thoughts, liberates your energy and inspires your hopes. Happiness is within you. It comes from doing some certain thing to which you can put all of your thought and energy. If you want to be happy get enthusiastic about something outside yourself."

The only way to lick an evil idea is with a greater idea. There are those who have set themselves to destroy us. Khrushchev said, "We will bury you." Their timetable calls for 1973 and many believe they are ahead of schedule. J. Frederic Dewhurst said in his book *America's Needs and Resources*: "Of all the great nations the one that clings most tenaciously to private capitalism has come closest to the socialistic goal of providing abundance for all in a classless society."

An interesting thing about our world is that in America today we have the purest example of what the fanatic false philosophies of communism seek to offer. Here about 7 per cent of the population live on farms and produce food for the other 93 per cent while in the Soviet Union it takes some 46 per cent of the people on farms to inadequately produce food for the rest. Furthermore the fantastic productive power of industry gives the average working man benefits that make him wealthy in comparison with what 90 per cent of the people of this world have. Of the total income in our nation less than 5 per cent is earned by those making $50,000 a year or more. Here under capitalism we have the two most precious possessions of all men—individual liberty and free enterprise, the pursuit of his goals to the benefit of others and to the satisfaction of his own needs.

Earl Nightingale tells the interesting story about a king in a European country who, as an experiment, took an aimless individual and put him in a cage, provided a warm bed and three good meals every day. For some time the man kept screaming, "Let me out. Why am I here? I've done nothing wrong." Then the king would come to see him each day and say to him, "Why you have nothing to worry about. You are warm in winter. You have no problems. All of your needs are met. You have adequate food. What else do you want?" Day after day he satisfied the sensate desires of this individual.

Finally one day a stranger passing by said, "Oh, that poor man, locked up in a cage. It must be terrible." The answer of the individual amazed him. He said, "I have everything—three good meals every day; no longer have to worry about working; I'm safe and protected; absolute security; everything I want I have right here." Was he successful? Tragically, terribly wasteful. No concern for his family. No interest in leaving an example of influence and inspiration to succeeding generations. No contribution to the social and spiritual needs of others. A slave. That's all he was.

How many people do you know like that who've never learned, much less enjoyed, the benefits of a dynamic goal?

Act now on setting a long-range goal. You can be successful, but there is no easy way to dynamic success.

Henry Ward Beecher has said, "Victories that are cheap are cheap. Those only are worth having which come as the result of hard fighting." Never forget those words, "What the mind can conceive and believe the mind can achieve."

Goethe, the German philosopher, said, "Before you can do something you must first be something." In other words you must act the part.

(1) Set one goal at a time—the goal that is most meaningful for you at this particular time.

(2) Think about it all the time. Build mind pictures of your achieving it. Use the five senses to bring your total personality to bear upon it.

(3) Drive it into your subconscious mind. Remember your subconscious mind takes orders. It is fantastically

creative. It never rests. Make your subconscious mind your willing servant by bringing to fruition the goal that you have set for it.

(4) Write out this goal in simple clear language.

By all means you will want to get and read and re-read the book by Napoleon Hill, *Think and Grow Rich*. Mr. Hill says that you should write out a goal. It should be simply stated. Something like this: From January 1, 1966, through December 31, 1970, I will receive $250,000. In return for this sum of money I will give undying loyalty to my firm, unquestioned faithfulness to my family, dedicated service to God through my church and the best program of personal improvement for myself possible. Such a goal as this will make you a dynamic individual. You can be successful.

You may wish to write a ten-year goal, then break it down into five-year segments. Certainly divide it into one-year periods and have monthly check-ups and weekly planning and a program of daily improvement. You see, you can be better than you think. It's all up to you. You usually use less than 10 per cent of your total mental power. You waste so many hours every day. You fret away in worry so much energy fruitlessly all because you didn't plan by setting a dynamic goal to achieve.

Yes, you *can* be successful. You *can* accomplish great things through the persistent achievement of a challenging worthy goal. Your key for personal success is through goals, but you must act now.

Goals Can Change Your Life

Goals, the check points on your journey of success:

1. What date do you expect to achieve the purpose you set for yourself earlier?

2. List changes in attitude, conduct, habits and associations necessary to reach this goal.

    A.

B.

C.

D.

3. Set up your goals in yearly segments from now until its realization.

4. Review these goals with your team, whether business or family to encourage their whole-hearted cooperation.

5. Commit yourself unswervingly to the accomplishment of these goals by printing them to post on the wall of your office, on calling cards or other places of daily contact. These are symbols that stimulate you to excel.

PART THREE
IMAGINATION

10. VIVID IMAGINATION

JOHN MASEFIELD said, "Man's body is faulty, his mind is untrustworthy, but his imagination has made him remarkable." Your key for personal success for today is imagination, the power and motivation of a magnificent mind, reaching beyond itself to scale heights never before imagined. Vivid imagination hunts for the ideal solution to life's problems and goals and then a dynamic imagination has the power to change what is found, to sift the information and bring the best results.

Two college presidents, Dr. Donald Cowling and Dr. Carter Davidson, say that the functions of the imaginative, creative mind are these: (1) Ability to concentrate. (2) Accuracy in observation. (3) Retentiveness of memory. (4) Logical reasoning. (5) Judgment. (6) Sensitivity of association. (7) Creative imagination.[1]

Seven Steps to Imagination

In the book *Applied Imagination,* Osborn[2] outlines the steps in the creative and productive imagination. (1) Orientation; pointing up the problem. (2) Preparation; gathering pertinent data. (3) Analysis; breaking down the relevant material. (4) Ideation; piling up alternatives by way of ideas. (5) Incubation; letting up, to invite illumination. (6) Synthesis; putting the pieces together. (7) Evaluation; judging the resultant ideas.

Dr. Maxwell Maltz in the book *Psycho-cybernetics* says: "Creative Imagination is not something reserved for the poets, the philosophers, the inventors, it enters into our every act, for imagination sets the goal, the picture which our automatic mechanism works on. We act, or fail to act not because of will as is so commonly believed but because of imagination.

---

[1]*Our Changing World,* No. 891.
[2]Alex Osborn, *Applied Imagination* (New York: Charles Scribner's Sons, 1953), page 115.

"A human being always acts and feels and performs in accordance with what he imagines to be true about himself and his environment."[3]

"Were it not for slow, painful and constantly discouraged creative effort," said James Harvey Robinson, "man would be no more than a species of primate living on seeds, fruits, roots and uncooked flesh."

Inventive Imagination

"It was imagination," said Victor Wagner, "that enabled man to extend his thumb by inventing the vise, to strengthen his fist and arm by inventing the hammer. Step by step man's imagination lured, led and often pushed him into the astonishing heights of power he now so apprehensively occupies."

An Imaginative Man

One of the truly imaginative men in business in America is Joseph Treadwell who in 1956, at thirty-two, became owner and manager of Treadwell Ford Agency, the downtown Ford dealer in Mobile, Alabama. Let me tell you about just a few of the things that Joe Treadwell does to stimulate business with his imaginative mind. Each November and December he has a Christmas tree on the sales floor. Everyone who buys a new Ford car during that two-month period receives a Christmas gift and he publicly advertises that this bag on the tree will have at least $101, maybe $1,000 or somewhere in between. You can imagine how people who are short of cash for Christmas would prefer buying a new Ford that will guarantee them at least a $101 for Christmas spending.

On other occasions he has given every purchaser of a new car a three-days-and-two-nights trip in the Smoky Mountains of East Tennessee at Gatlinburg, or he may give them a three-days-and-two-nights trip with all expenses paid to Miami Beach. Again he has given a barrel of gas with every car, that is fifty-five gallons of free gasoline. On occasions he has loaded up all of his salesmen in the black hearse that he bought and has taken them out to shopping centers where they will go around and place,

---

[3]Maltz, *Ibid.*, page 28.

"Will you take (a certain amount)?" on the windshield of the automobiles.

He has advertised, "Buy a Ford from the man in the red coat" and every salesman wore a bright red coat, a bright red hat and carried a red walking cane. On other occasions he has had fifty common carriers with four, five or six Fords on each one all together with big signs saying, "Trade at Treadwell Ford. I'm going to Treadwell Ford." Imagine fifty truck loads of Fords all led by police motorcycle escort going criss-crossing through the downtown streets of the city of Mobile before they wind up at Treadwell. He has gigantic fish fries and invites the public to join him.

On a billboard in a prominent location in the city he has raised a brand new Ford automobile and has hired a model at $100 a week, three hours in the morning and three hours in the afternoon. She sat in the car or stood by the car up on the billboard waving to the people as they drove by.

He put a tall acid jug on the sales floor and every time he caught a salesman not smiling he made him put at least ten cents in the acid jar.

To stimulate his associates he does many things. On one occasion he sent a box filled with crumpled bills and with a note saying that all the taxes were paid on it. Inside this box were one thousand three wadded up $1.00 bills and one five dollar bill. He gave it as a gift to his general manager. People in the automobile industry all over America know how imaginative Joe Treadwell is. It pays off. At least 2,000 new Fords are sold every year.

Meditative Moments

Many ask, "Well, how good is imagination? Isn't it all daydreams?" Samuel Johnson has said, "Many have no happier moments than those that they pass in solitude, abandoned to their own imagination, which sometimes puts sceptres in their hands or miters on their heads, shifts the scene of pleasure with endless variety, bids all the forms of beauty sparkle before them, and gluts them with every change of visionary luxury." But is this what imagination really is? I think not. Certainly, creative imagination dreams, but productive imagination furnishes the dreams to the wheels of reality.

"Imagination rules the world." —Napoleon.

"Imagination is more important than knowledge." — Albert Einstein.

"Imagination makes man the master of animals." — Shakespeare.

"Imagination governs the world." —Disraeli.

Let's study this important dynamic of life's fullness further.

11. IMAGINATION DEFINED

YOUR KEY for personal success is imagination. What is imagination? We are studying how you can be an imaginative, dynamic, outstanding individual.

I think the best definition of what imagination does is from Dugald Stewart, "The faculty of imagination is the great spring of human activity, and the principal source of human improvement. As it delights in presenting to the mind scenes and characters more perfect than those which we are acquainted with, it prevents us from ever being completely satisfied with our present condition and with our past attainments and engages us continually in the pursuit of some untried enjoyment or of some ideal excellence. Destroy this faculty and the condition of man will become as stationary as that of the brutes." And the Bard of Stratford on Avon, William Shakespeare, said, "The poet's eye, in a fine frenzy rolling, Doth glance from heaven to earth, from earth to heaven; And as imagination bodies forth The forms of things unknown, the poet's pen Turns them to shapes, and gives to airy nothing A local habitation and a name. Such tricks hath strong imagination. . . ."

Three Laws of Association

The key to creative imagination is association. Dr. Alex Osborn in his book *Applied Imagination* said that association is developed by the three laws of the Greeks discovered for us[1]: First, contiguity. This means nearness, as

---

[1] Osborn, *Ibid.*, pages 110-112.

when a baby's shoe reminds you of an infant. Contiguous means touching, in contact with, or in close proximity without actually touching, or near. For example, a dictaphone says to me "executive" and a successful executive because the successful executive is one who's conservative of his time and knows that with the use of the dictaphone he can produce more.

The second law of association is similarity in that the picture of a lion will remind you of a cat. The metaphor implies similarity. Allegories, fables and parables are likewise founded on similarities. For example, a happy child will remind you of home or of parents but it also may suggest a new opportunity, such as the new year brings.

Third, association is accomplished by contrast. For example, a midget might remind you of a giant or a hobo might remind you of a millionaire.

Audio Association

Association also works through sound. The song, "A Pretty Girl Is Like a Melody" reminds me of a beautiful recording of that song with a soprano obligato that I played on numerous occasions while a disc jockey with an armed forces radio station in Tsingtao, China, immediately after World War II. It was the most popular song the marines and sailors called for.

Of course combination is the essence of creativity, Dr. Easton has said, "A creative thinker evolves no new ideas. He actually evolves new combinations of ideas that are already in his mind."

Our actions through our life are the result of associations with earlier convictions, ideas and beliefs. For example Cecil B. DeMille, who produced so many of the great Bible motion pictures, said: "I have no doubt that my father's vivid reading of Biblical stories planted in my impressionable mind a reverence and respect for the Bible, perhaps even a sense of its dramatic value, which in subsequent years was to turn me to the Great Book for themes to thrill motion picture audiences." How many times have you been discussing something with someone when they suddenly said, "Hey, that gives me an idea."

I've often found that my most creative times have been while hearing someone else speak. I make it a rigid rule never to go to hear someone else speak, whether at a convention, church, civic club, or whatever without taking my note pad with me, for many times, in fact on most occasions, I get ideas from things that were said. "Ideas are flighty things. That which now seems perfectly clear may later get away from you. Make a habit of jotting down ideas as they occur to you. Although many of them will not work out they may suggest other thoughts."—Daymon Aiken.

Your imagination is vividly activated through creative association with other ideas. You can be successful.

12. BRAINSTORMING

YOUR KEY to personal success is imagination, and you develop your imagination by brainstorming. Brainstorming is simply using the brain power of a compatible group to storm a problem. There are two-way values of brainstorming. (1) It automatically excites the individual's own imagination. (2) It stimulates the associate power of all others present. It brings out their best. It challenges them to think creatively.

"When you really get going in a brainstorming session a spark from one's mind will light up a lot of bang-up ideas in the others just like a string of fire crackers." —Fred Sharpe.

The results of brainstorming are truly amazing. The United States Treasury has found that it secured 103 good ideas in 40 minutes on the subject, "How can we get more Federal employees to sell more United States Savings Bonds?" They received eighty-nine ideas in thirty minutes on the subject, "How to reduce absenteeism." My experience has been that you often get the best results in a shorter period of time. Sometimes it bogs down after fifteen or twenty minutes. Then stop and rest for awhile and come back with a fresh approach or a new problem.

What are the principles of brainstorming? Alex Osborn discusses them[1]: Ideation can be more productive if criticism is concurrently excluded. Don't undermine any

---

[1] Osborn, *Ibid.*, pages 156-158.

creative idea. If you pause to criticize someone else's idea you lose the initiative and creativity of your own. Furthermore it breaks the positive thought of the entire group. It also creates hostility and divides the group. No adverse judgment of ideas should be allowed.

"If you try to get hot and cold water out of the same faucet at the same time you will get only tepid water. And if you try to criticize and create at the same time you can't turn on either cold enough criticism or hot enough ideas. So let's stick solely to ideas. Let's cut out all criticism during the session of brainstorming." —Alex Osborn.

Free Wheeling

The second basic rule in brainstorming is that free wheeling is welcomed—the wilder the ideas the better. Your wild idea may bring forth a ready response, a constructive gem from someone else. Remember it is easier to tone down than to think up. Let the crazy ideas come and speak the first thought that comes to your mind. It may be a jewel.

The More the Better

Quantity is important. The more ideas the better. The greater the number, the more likely a winner. It has been found that the last fifty ideas produced at a brainstorming session have averaged higher in quality than the first fifty. Quantity breeds quality.

Creative Power

The fourth principle is a combination: improvement comes as a result of brainstorming. Other participants may improve upon your idea, creating a much better suggestion. Remember group ideation is far more productive than individual ideation.

Remember also that brainstorming is fun. The two guides to the success of a brainstorming group are: (1) How many good ideas did you find later? (2) Did the group enjoy it? Good brainstorming really is an enjoyable event. If it's done at work you will find the people may feel a bit guilty being paid for having a wonderful time. What's wrong with that?

In dozens of experiences of brainstorming in church groups, economic groups and social groups I have found that the leader is the key. If the leader will state a positive idea, be firm about the rules of brainstorming, set a definite time limit, stop at the end of the time limit, make it a game—a joyful experience—don't let them tire, rest or take up other subjects, you will find it to be a great and tremendous experience.

Judge Ideas Later

Once you have received the ideas do not grade them or judge them. Let a committee or individual do it at a later time. You may want to use a dictating machine or a tape recorder or have a secretary take the ideas down in shorthand. Be sure that you get *all* of the ideas. What seems unimportant at the time may later prove to be valuable.

Imagination is a gold mine. How much better if you have a number of gold mines going for you! Brainstorm your way to success.

13. CREATIVE LEISURE

YOUR KEY for personal success today is imagination, and your imagination is at its best in leisure ideation. It has been found that in testing 702 individuals, women are 25 per cent more creative than men. Why do you suppose this is true? Isn't it for the very same reason that women live longer? Women are more creative and live longer because they break the strains of the day in leisure activity. They do not work at the same frenzy as the man who is at the office or laying bricks or selling, therefore their physical body rests more and their minds are more productive and more creative.

Creativity in Leisure

How many times have you been on the golf course when the idea came that solved the problem at the office? How many times have you been driving down the highway and suddenly, out of the blue, the solution came? Your conscious mind had been telling your subconscious mind for a long while that you had a problem and your subconscious mind was at work on it. In leisure, when the intensity of the conscious effort is relaxed, the subconscious mind takes over. Then when you are ready to listen to the subconscious mind suddenly the idea is consciously placed before you.

Your Idea Hot House

The word incubation indicates intentional relaxation. In medicine it refers to the phase in the development of an infectious disease between infection and the first symptom. In imagination it means the relaxed atmosphere by which we let our subconscious mind bring to consciousness the solution to our problems.

Dr. Hornall Hart, professor emeritus at Duke University says, "Pay attention to your hunches. I even pay attention to my wife's, they are better than mine." When we are relaxed these flashes come seemingly out of nowhere but literally they are the response of a creative mind. They are not mere freak phenomena to be examined as curiosities. When our bodies are as relaxed as a sack of flour these flashes are more readily before us.

Harry Hepner, professor of psychology at Syracuse University, said, "The appearance of a good idea seemingly comes from nowhere.... Failure to record the flash or to follow it through may entail a tragic inability to do so later." Ralph Waldo Emerson encouraged us to "Look sharply after your thoughts. They come unlooked for like a new bird seen in your trees and if you turn to your usual task they disappear."

My personal experience reveals that many times a thought, an idea or a message, address, or a sermon, comes suddenly out of the blue. I always keep a notebook in hand and I write down these thoughts and I keep the notebook with me at all times. In a moment of leisure again a further development of the thought comes, an illustration here, a humorous anecdote there, and the body of the message springs into view. This is incubation.

Let It Simmer

Edna Ferber wrote, "A story must simmer in its own juice for months or even years before it is ready to serve."

Remarked Constance Robertson, "I have found that it pays to hold a plot in suspension and not to worry it or force it. At the right point I go into a long lull. Then I tackle my typewriter and write whatever comes. My story then seems to reel itself off in a most extraordinary way." This was the key to Edison. Most of us know that he would go for days and not go home to sleep, but few people knew that he had a sofa in his office and he would catnap there from time to time. Here some of his most outstanding ideas came into being. Here his creative mind brought forth the so-called flashes of ingenuity.

Lowell Thomas recommends a prescription from Yoga which calls for a deliberate, sustained period of silence— just an hour of silence, sitting still, neither reading nor looking upon anything in particular.

Furthermore do not be a rigid slave driver. Flit from one idea to another. You will find that the truly outstanding ideas will keep coming back to you from time to time. Play these hunches as an organist plays all of the console to bring forth the tremendous tunes from all the pipes.

One time of challenging ideation for me is in worship. When hearing the minister bring forth the message, whether in convention or in church, I have found some amazing and seemingly miraculous solutions to problems that have been confronting me before.

Dr. Norman Vincent Peale holds that for creative meditation "there is nothing like peace-drenched mountains with their deep, sun-bathed pensive valleys. Here our minds clear and our ability to think creatively returns."

Of course, the best leisure ideation comes during periods of rest following conscious work.

Add Years to Your Life

Furthermore a definite value of leisure ideation is in lengthening your life. A recent study at the University of Chicago reveals that men who think creatively actually are young at fifty and appear to be aging slowly but men who work with their hands seem to be old at fifty and are aging rapidly.

So let me urge you through conscious effort to plant the seeds of knowledge, of suggestion, of information, of fact and trust the fabulous power of your creative mind to bring you the solution during leisure ideation. Leave your desk. Go to the golf course. Go out on the ocean fishing or in your lake nearby. Work in your garden. Spend time at your stamp collection or whatever it is that you enjoy doing. Get away from the tedious and leisurely enjoy life. In doing so you are not wasting time; you are using it to the best of your ability.

14. HINDRANCES OF IMAGINATION

YOUR KEY to personal success is imagination. You can become an imaginative, creative person. But these are hindrances to creative imagination. Italian Zoologist Battista Grassi has divided mankind into three classes: (1) Those who work with their minds. (2) Those who pretend to do so. (3) Those who do neither. "Unless you are in the first class," said Grassi, "you will probably fail to summon up the energy to make yourself do the things you have to do to get the most out of your imagination."

Daydreams Are Deadly

The first hindrance is daydreaming. I'm speaking here of idle and purposeless fantasy. Dreams with no roots, dreams with no reality—these are hindrances. Truly creative dreams are the solution to, as well as the desire of, our aspirations and goals in life.

Psychiatrist Freud said, "Every neurosis has the result and therefore probably the purpose of forcing the patient out of real life, of alienating him from actuality." This then is the weakness of daydreams that have no root nor purpose, no plan nor goal in life. They destroy rather than build up.

James Russell Lowell has said, "Solitude is as needful to the imagination as society is wholesome for the character." We are not talking about the leisure ideation that solitude brings. This is wonderfully creative. We are talking about the unreal, impractical, irrational daydreaming that leads an individual to escape from the reality of purpose and actually is a division of the mind.

The Morbid Movie of Worry

The second hindrance to imagination is worry. This is Public Enemy No 1. More people have been destroyed and are being destroyed every year by worry than any other single cause. The Bible says, "Ye cannot serve God and mammon." You cannot serve two masters at once. Neither can you be an enthusiastic, vibrant, alert, creative individual and be saturated with the viciousness of worry. Worry is corrosive, corruptive and destructive. Dr. Harry Fosdick has labeled it "anxious fear." He says, "Worry is like running reels of morbid movies through our minds." Therefore we must change reels. We must run the reel of vibrant purpose, of joyful living, of enthusiastic endeavor, of dynamic purpose, then we will destroy the hindrance of worry.

How to Battle the Blues

The blues are the third hindrance to imagination. At breakfast one morning a lady is supposed to have said to her husband, "I'm down in the dumps. I believe I'll go buy a new hat." Her husband replied, "So that's where you've been getting them."

Recent scientific studies reveal that everyone has both a high peak of emotional intensity and a low level of emotional discouragement each thirty-day period. If you let the blues master you there will come a time when you will be in a constant thirty-day period of deep and decided depression. There are some positive things that we can do to overcome the blues. Let me suggest some that I have practiced. I keep in my office a stereo record player with some of the finest music. When I am discouraged I play the music, turn it up high so that the whole vibrancy of the exhilarating strains will drive my moods of despair into the ground and lift me up to heights of joy. I have a record player in my car that is connected to the radio, and when I can't get good radio music I turn on *Music Man, South Pacific, Oklahoma,* semi-classical and classical numbers that lift me to emotional heights. Another way to whip worry is to enjoy the presence in spirited conversation of exhilarating people. We become what the crowd we run with is. Be with enthusiastic people and you will be enthusiastic.

Another way to whip worry is to spend some creative

hours with your favorite hobby. You will find that this will bring new spirit, new vision, new outlook and help you to lift the dread disease of worry. Remember to make the blues your slave not your master.

Total Mind Control

Evil thoughts are the fourth hindrance to imagination. Charles Haddon Spurgeon said, "A vile imagination, once indulged, gets the key of our minds, and can get in again very easily, whether we will or no, and can so return as to bring seven other spirits with it even more wicked than itself; and what may follow no one knows." F. W. Robertson, another great English cleric, has said, "Imagination enobles appetites which in themselves are low, and spiritualizes acts which, else, are only animal. . . . But the pleasures which begin in the senses only sensualize."

Remember there is only one principle that all philosophers of all ages have agreed upon, and that is this, "We become what we think about." "As a man thinketh in his heart so is he." Show me what a man is thinking and I will tell you where he will be a few years from now. Our senses should be the servants and slaves that lead us to outstanding success. Remember the greatest success is he who performs the greatest service for the most of mankind. Don't make the senses your god. Make the service of God and mankind your purpose and then you've really begun to live.

Overcome the hindrances to imagination. Be your own master. Don't let daydreams, worry, the blues and evil thoughts drive you to despair. You can be successful. Become so today.

15. DEVELOPING IMAGINATION

YOUR KEY for personal success is imagination. How can you develop an imaginative mind? You can be successful. One of the best ways to develop your imagination is to simply force yourself to work at it. George Meyer, when asked how he turned out the song *For Me and My Gal*, snapped back, "I just sat down and went to work." Clarence

Budington Kelland, a prolific fiction writer, confesses that he would hardly turn out anything if he didn't force himself to work each morning immediately after breakfast whether he feels in the mood or not.

Here are two ways to get started:

(1) Concentrate. Focalize your psychic energy upon one goal. Write out your purpose. Intensify your efforts upon it. Stay with it. Bring all the power, the experience, the background, the facts and the knowledge you can accumulate upon that one purpose. Spend time meditating on it.

(2) Then team up with a compatible group, collaborate with others who will help you accomplish it. A great man delights in helping others. I have found that the more successful a man is the more helpful he will be to others. He wants to share his knowledge with others, particularly younger people. Therefore go to outstanding people round about you. Call upon them, their knowledge, their background and their experience. Ask them to help you in achieving this purpose. You will be amazed how readily they will reply.

In his book *How To Win Success Before Forty* Damroth tells how to make ideas pay off.[1] (1) We must apply idea ability to the job. (2) Let your ideas flow freely, be a wildcatter. (3) Concentrate on the big idea. (4) Don't quit until your idea is a reality. Stay with it.

Make Your Moods Your Servants

Alex Osborn says we need to establish a working mood. He suggests this is similar to pulling ourselves up by a boot strap. Even self-confidence can be self-induced to some extent. As a baseball player swings two bats before stepping up to the plate we need to flex our imagination when approaching a creative task. Osborn tells of ad writer Allen Ward, who accomplishes amazing results in ideation. Listen to Ward's formula: "I have no sure way of uninhibiting myself for creative thinking, but I've found that one good way to get into a working mood is to close my door and try to forget everything but the job before me. Then I pull my typewriter to me, wrap my legs around it and start to write. I write down every line that

---

[1] William G. Damroth, *How To Win Success Before Forty* (Englewood Cliffs, N.J.: Prentice-Hall, Inc., 1956), page 91.

comes into my head—crazy, dull or however it sounds. I find that if I don't it may linger there and block others. I write as fast as I can. Then after a long while some cogs that haven't worked start to whir and something striking begins to type itself out on the yellow sheet before me like a telegraph message. That's the hard way and about the only way I know."

Some of the world's most outstanding writers have been those who have known firsthand the experiences they relate. Certainly Hemingway lived his experiences. He wrote of his experiences. Therefore, the more varied our experience the more definite our imagination. Of course we can increase this imagination and make it firsthand experience by reading. Become a prolific reader. Develop your reading rate. I have had for many years a reading rate machine that has more than doubled my reading rate. The late President John F. Kennedy was able to digest an amazing amount of reports because he could read at 1200 words a minute. He literally had developed his reading rate to a phenomenal amount. Read biographies. Read constructive fantasies. Read books of faith and inspiration. And by all means read the Bible.

Act Out Your Success Role

You can develop imagination by role playing. Imagine yourself in the shoes of a particular person. Imagine yourself as President of the United States. Begin at the first hour in the morning and imagine yourself through every conference, through every meeting, through every council activity, through every telephone call, through every responsibility during the day. Play the role of that person. You will be able to imagine yourself in his very shoes.

This is especially helpful if you are selling. Imagine yourself in the shoes of the purchasing agent that you are calling upon. Find out about the problems that he is facing. Set out to serve him and his company by proving that you have the solution. Then you are his ally, you're his friend, you're his associate; you aren't someone competing for his time, you're one who is there to help him. Imagination places yourself in his shoes through role playing.

Then finally let me urge you to practice mental pictures in achieving imaginative goals. Harry Emerson Fosdick said, "Hold a picture of yourself long and steadily enough in your mind's eye and you will be drawn toward it. Picture yourself vividly as defeated and that alone will make victory impossible. Picture yourself vividly as winning and that alone will contribute immeasurably to success. Great living starts with a picture, held in your imagination, of what you would like to do or to be."

I have a life-insurance salesman friend in Missouri who will someday become a $75,000 a year vice-president with his nationally-known insurance company. He is playing the role. He has pictured himself there. He is taking every possible means of personal improvement. He is paying the price of long hours, of diligent work. He is a cooperative team member. It is inevitable that he will be the vice-president of that firm, or maybe the president.

Produce and Star in our Own Movie

Imagine yourself sitting before a large motion picture screen. You are on the screen. The important thing you see in these pictures is a vivid and detailed projection of the person you want to become. See yourself moving about that screen, achieving the very things that you are dreaming of. Earl Nightingale says this is one of the best ways to lose weight. Picture your slim self walking across that motion picture screen with all the vitality of life that can truly be yours. Spend a little time each day, an increasing amount of time as each day goes by, picturing yourself on that motion picture screen, the truly successful, dynamic individual you wish to become. Napoleon practiced soldiering in his imagination for many years before he actually went on the battlefield. Webb and Morgan in their book *Making the Most of Your Life* tell us, "The notes Napoleon made from his readings during these years of study filled, when printed, 400 pages. He imagined himself as a commander and drew maps of the islands of Corsica showing where he would place various defenses, making all of his calculations with mathematical precision."[2]

Conrad Hilton imagined himself operating a hotel long before he ever bought one. As a boy he used to play that he was a hotel operator. Henry Kaiser has said that each of his business accomplishments was realized in his imagi-

---

[2] *Our Changing World*, No. 747.

nation before it appeared in actuality. Dr. Albert Edward Wiggam called mental picturing of yourself "the strongest force within you."

Dr. Leslie Weatherhead has said, "If we have in our minds a picture of ourselves as fear haunted and defeated nobodies we must get rid of that picture at once and hold up our heads. That is a false picture and the false must go. God sees us as men and women in whom and through whom He can do a great work. He sees us as already serene, confident and cheerful. He sees us not as pathetic victims of life, but masters of the art of living; not wanting sympathy, but imparting help to others and therefore thinking less and less of ourselves and full, not of self-concern, but of love and laughter and a desire to serve."[3]

Imagination

You are successful the moment you imagine your purpose:

1. Imagine yourself in the act of accomplishing your purpose. Use the five senses to place yourself at the moment of achievement.

For instance, say that your purpose is to build a $500,-000 building at your alma mater named for your parents.

A. Can you see yourself projected across the screen of your mind through imagination in the very act of handing the keys to the President of the College? Visualize the building—red brick, white columns. two stories, etc.

B. Can you smell the flowers on the speaker's stand, the corsages worn by the ladies present and the special bouquet handed to your mother?

C. Can you taste the joy of achievement, realizing that thousands of students will respond to life's highest challenges as a result of your gift?

---

[3]Osborn, *Ibid.*, page 149.

D. Can you hear the band playing in the background, the burst of applause, the deep and sincere words of appreciation from a faculty, alumni and students?

E. Can you feel the key in your left hand, the President's warm handclasp in your right in the very act of presentation?

2. Now make your purpose come alive by writing out below your crowning event of a lifetime using the five senses.

3. Schedule brainstorming sessions with each compatible group that can help you achieve your purpose. Remember big men delight in accomplishing glorious things.

PART FOUR
BUILD CONFIDENCE AND SUCCEED

16. WHIP WORRY

ONE WOMAN'S way of dealing with worry was, "I've joined the new Don't Worry Club and now I hold my breath. I'm so afraid I'll worry that I'm worried half to death." Your key for personal success is building personal, individual self-confidence by whipping worry.

John Edmund Haggai in his book *How to Win Over Worry*[1] says that worry is Public Enemy No. 1. He says that mental illness is costing this nation two-and-a-half billion dollars a year; that many more Americans commit suicide (the result of stress, duress, anxiety and worry) than die from the five most common communicable diseases. For instance, in 1957, 220 people died of polio, 15,980 committed suicide. Seventy-five hundred more people committed suicide than were victims of homicide. A total of 10,170 people died as a result of ulcers. At least 17,000,000 Americans are suffering from some form of mental illness. During World War II more than 300,000 of America's finest young men were killed in combat. During the same period of time over a million civilians died from heart disease, primarily the result of worry. One doctor states that worry causes heart trouble, high blood pressure, some forms of asthma, rheumatism, ulcers, colds, thyroid malfunction, arthritis, migraine headaches, blindness and a host of stomach disorders in addition to ulcers.

You cannot have confidence until you whip worry.

What People Worry About

Notice these statistics about things people worry about: Things that never happen, 40 per cent; things they can't change, 30 per cent; needless worry about health, 12 per cent; petty and miscellaneous worrying, 10 per cent; real

---

[1]John Edmund Haggai, *How To Win Over Worry* (Grand Rapids, Mich.: Zondervan Publishing House, 1959), pages 15, 16.

problems, 8 per cent. Therefore 92 per cent of the things people worry about are ruinous and uncontrollable. Furthermore worrying is sin, for it not only destroys man's health but even can cause him to commit suicide. Phillips translates Philippians 4:6-8 thusly, "Don't worry over anything whatever; tell God every detail of your needs in earnest and thankful prayer, and the peace of God, which transcends human understanding, will keep constant guard over your hearts and minds as they rest in Christ Jesus. Here is a last piece of advice. If you believe in goodness and if you value the approval of God, fix your minds on whatever is true and honorable and just and pure and lovely and praiseworthy."[2]

Davidson, in his book *How I Discovered the Secret of Success in the Bible*,[3] tells how to build confidence: "(1) You must know your product. Know what you are doing. Master your job. (2) You must avoid all exaggerations. You must practice the art of understatement rigorously and conscientiously. (3) You must be willing and able to prove your case with facts developed from several different angles. (4) You must present your case in a tone of quiet authority without apology or uncertainty." Then, there is nothing to worry about. You have all the facts. You have people's confidence and friendship. You are then whipping worry.

Worry Produces Nervous Breakdowns

Dan Custer[4] says that worry is the interest we pay on trouble before it is due. It never solved any problem. It is completely destructive and disintegrating. Still, many of us continue to indulge in it. Worry is a malfunction of the mind. The wrong use of the mind results in disease. Therefore, worrying is against the law. The Buddhists say, "The two devils of the emotional kingdom are anger and fear. Anger, the brain passion, and fear the freezing passion." The Apostle Paul said, "God has not given us the spirit of fear; but of power, and of love, and of a sound

[2]J. B. Phillips, *The New Testament in Modern English* (New York: The Macmillan Company, 1958).

[3]Clinton Davidson, *How I Discovered the Secret of Success From the Bible* (Westwood, N.J.: Revell, 1964), page 50.

[4]Dan Custer, *The Miracle of Mind Power* (Englewood Cliffs, N.J.: Prentice-Hall, Inc., 1960), pages 220-221.

mind."[5] We are not born with fear. It is a cultivated mental disease that destroys. Therefore, a sound mind is an integrated mind—a mind in one piece; a mind working harmoniously together. When worry controls the mind it leads to abulia, or loss of the power of the will, because the mind is divided and cannot act in one channel. Abulia is often a nervous breakdown. This literally means divided mindness. The victim has quit struggling and yields to a depressed and passive manner. Worrying is injurious to the human body. Furthermore, it is injurious to social fellowship, and to business relations and family affairs. Worry is suicidal.

In the Thirty-Seventh Psalm David wrote, "Trust in the Lord, and do good; so shalt thou dwell in the land, and verily thou shalt be fed." The way to whip worry is to crowd worry out of your mind with positive spiritual thoughts.

Forgive Yourself

Over more than a dozen years of counseling with people who had many problems, I have found that a guilt complex has brought more worry and emotional destruction than most any other thing. The person with a guilt complex has never learned to forgive himself. Therefore he is punishing himself. When you punish yourself you are violating life's most important and most dynamic motivating principle—self-preservation. Such action comes from a puritanical, religious atmosphere on the part of some and a fear of punishment on the part of God by others. The nature of God is forgiveness. In I John 1:9 we have the passage, "If we confess our sins, he is faithful and just to forgive us our sins, and to cleanse us from all unrighteousness." Learn to forgive yourself so you then can whip worry.

Dr. John A. Schindler[6] writes about the dangers and destructive powers of E.I.I., emotionally induced illness. He says that over 50 per cent of those seeking medical aid have it. In a thousand different cases emotionally induced illness is as common as all of the other 999 diseases put together. Dr. Schindler reports that at the Oschsner Clinic

---

[5]II Timothy 1:7.
[6]John A. Schindler, *How to Live 365 Days a Year* (Englewood Cliffs, N.J.: Prentice-Hall, Inc., 1954), pages 3-4.

in New Orleans they found that 74 per cent of 500 consecutive patients admitted to the department handling gastro-intestinal diseases were found to be suffering from E.I.I. In 1951, a paper from the Yale University Out-Patient Medical Department indicated that 76 per cent of patients coming to that clinic were suffering from E.I.I.

These people literally were worrying themselves to death.

An Emotion Greater Than Worry

There is one other emotion that is just as dynamic as worry. Worry is dangerous to every crowd, for the one who worries contaminates all the others round about. But here is another contagious solution. It is enthusiasm—the vital quality that arouses you to action. Self-control is the balance wheel that directs your action and will lead you to be positive and powerful and overcome the destructiveness of worry.

To be a well-rounded, well-adjusted, well-balanced individual you must have self-control and enthusiasm. Remember, there is only one thing in all this world that you hold total control over and that is your mind. You can master worry. You can whip worry by the positive power of enthusiasm. You see, you are the sum total of your dominating and most prominent thoughts.

For example, if your family is having a discussion—let's say you are involved in an argument. You have raised your voices in disagreement. The doorbell rings. Immediately the entire family stops talking. You do not want to be embarrassed in front of visitors. So you crowd out the emotion of disunity and you put on a front for the visitors. In the same way you can crowd out the emotion of worry and instill in its place enthusiasm, positive thinking and personal self-confidence.

Harold Sherman tells an interesting story of the positive power of P. T. Barnum, the great showman.[7] Once awakened from a sound sleep in the middle of the night he was told, "Mr. Barnum, one quarter of the circus has been completely destroyed by fire." Barnum sat up, blinking his eyes. "What are you going to do?" asked the messenger, expecting Barnum to leap from the bed and start issuing

---

[7]Harold Sherman, *How to Turn Failure Into Success* (Englewood Cliffs, N.J.: Prentice-Hall, Inc., 1958), pages 22-23.

orders. "I can do nothing tonight," Mr. Barnum replied, "so I'm going back to sleep." There you have it With confidence. he had learned to whip worry.

Crowd worry out with enthusiastic action. Forgive yourself, for guilt feelings deny creativity and strength. Face the fact that worry always destroys. It never helps.

17. FIGHT FEAR

YOUR KEY for success today is to fight fear with faith and with facts. You can be a self-confident, triumphant, successful individual.

Napoleon Hill says that there are seven basic fears: "(1) The fear of poverty. (2) The fear of criticism. (3) The fear of ill health. (4) The fear of loss of love. (5) The fear of old age. (6) The fear of loss of liberty. (7) The fear of death."[1] Let's build self-confidence in fighting these fears.

We must fight fear with facts. Emerson has said, "Trust thyself, every breast vibrates to that iron string of trust." When your mind and message is filled with facts you become a radiant dynamic individual.

In Carl Sandburg's book, *Abraham Lincoln: The Prairie Years,* we have this illustration: "A listener to one of Abraham Lincoln's speeches gives the picture. 'As his body loosened and swayed to the cadence of his address and as his thoughts unfolded drops of sweat stood out on his forehead; he was speaking not only with his tongue but with every blood drop of his body.' A scholarly man said, 'His manner was impassioned and he seemed transfigured; his listeners felt that he believed every word he said and that like Martin Luther he would go to the stake rather than abate one jot or tittle of it.' "[2]

Now let's look at the facts. What is the worst possible

---

[1]Hill, *Think and Grow Rich,* page 82.
[2]Carl Sandburg, *Abraham Lincoln: The Prairie Years* (New York: Harcourt-Brace and Company, 1926), page 72.

thing that could happen to you? Put your mind in reverse for a moment and let's just anticipate—loss of health or job, whatever it is. What would you do if that were to occur? Sit down and write out a course of action, step by step. Next, plan to make the best of that worst possible thing, perhaps even use it for improvement (such as getting a better job). When you face the fact that the worst that could happen to you can be dealt with, and that it is unlikely to occur in the first place, you can revel in the joy of life's pleasures and achievements.

Take Your Own Inventory

Play up your good points. Just sit down and make an inventory. In the left-hand column list all of your faults and failures. In the right-hand column positively, carefully and honestly list all of your good features—pleasing personality, good education, fine family background, etc. Unless you are neurotic, you will find yourself way ahead of the game.

In one of his radio addresses Earl Nightingale refers to a quote by Balzac: "By resorting to self-resignation the unfortunate consummate their misfortunes." As long as the followers of Mohammed have predominately in their teaching, "Allah wills it" and this fatalistic philosophy, the people of that state will never dominate the world by thoughts, their philosophy, or their leadership. But we have followers of fatalism here. Such statements: "Well, that's the way things go." "That's the way the cookie crumbles." "That's the way the ball bounces." Now if this statement is a dismissal of a mistake or misfortune, then all right, but too often it is the destruction of initiative. Frank Pierce says that by facing the facts you control your destiny to a great extent.

Fight Fear with Faith. Fear is amazingly contagious. One person can infect and ruin otherwise amiable relationships. Fear hampers our ability to think and to reason effectively. Extreme fear can paralyze our capacity to act. Fear even increases pain. It is known that 75 per cent of pain that is felt while a person is tense and jittery will disappear when a person is totally relaxed. Don't try to flee from your fears; face them with a positive faith. Admit them, but crowd them out with faith. Open the closet of your mind. Grab the fears in the dark recesses. Hold them out into the sunlight of God's love and truth and trample them into the dust. Levy has said, "A person under the firm persuasion that he can command resources virtually has them."

Napoleon Hill commented on this subject, "Is it not strange that we fear most that which never happens; that we destroy our initiative by the fear of defeat when in reality defeat is the most useful tonic and it should be accepted as such."

You fight fear with faith and with facts by acting the part of confidence, by getting all of the information. Right at this moment determine that you will not be the victim of fear, but you will be the victor with faith. You will not let fear frustrate and ruin your present and your future. You will not fail to fight. And, furthermore, don't contaminate other healthy positive minds by the contagion of fear. If you will not be victor, then go like a hermit to a cave in isolation of your own defeat. But you do not have to do that. You can be victor.

18. DOMINATE DOUBTS

YOUR KEY to confidence is to dominate your doubts. Shakespeare has said, "Our doubts are traitors and make us lose the good we oft might win by fearing to attempt." Doubts are good when they can be controlled. Doubts are good when they lead us to a keen evaluation. Gathering the facts, and seriously studying the situation, help bring caution and wisdom. Only fools never have doubts.

But a great majority of people let their doubts rule them. You must admit your inadequacies to overcome doubt. Face the fact that you do not excel in everything. Acknowledge that you have weaknesses. In the very process of admitting your inadequacies you dominate your doubts. See, a problem well stated is half solved. When a person can face the fact that he is inadequate in a certain area, that person will go and find help somewhere. This is the way to dominate your doubts. You are more important than the emotion of doubt. Samuel Johnson has said that "Nothing will ever be attempted if all possible objections must first be overcome."

Let the doubt give you wisdom; let the doubt be satisfied; let the doubt raise its head and then when maturity, wisdom, experience, and knowledge have led you to realize that the doubt is satisfied, move on. According to Shakespeare, "Modest doubt is called the beacon of the wise—the tent that searches to the bottom of the worst."

The trouble is that many people do not have modest doubts. They have magnificent, mountainous doubts that crush them.

Don't Let Doubts Destroy You

Remember that doubts are destructive. They destroy action. They tear up the peace and serenity and happiness of a man's life. Listen to Robert South, English clergyman and author: "There is no weariness like that which rises from doubting—from the perpetual jogging of unfixed reason. The torment of suspense is very great; but as soon as the wavering, perplexed mind begins to determine, be the determination which way soever it may be, it will find itself at ease."

Eliminate your doubts by speaking your convictions. Don't be a Mr. Milquetoast. "The man who speaks his positive convictions is worth a regiment of men who are always proclaiming their doubts and suspicions," said Pliney the Elder. Daniels, a mountain philosopher from Tennessee, used to say, "Don't figger how you can't; figger how you can." So gather the facts and act. Don't wait. Dominate, dictate, control your doubts. P. T. Munger so well said, "Knowledge and personality make doubt possible. But knowledge is also the cure of doubt; and when we get a full and adequate sense of personality we are lifted into a region where doubt is almost impossible, for no man can know himself as he is, in all the fulness of his nature, without also knowing God."

Your Pause That Refreshes

Doubt should be the "pause that refreshes" on the pathway to personal success. But don't let the "coke break" last all day. Don't let the five-minute period stretch into four hours. This truth is expressed by English clergyman Caleb Colton when he said, "Doubt is the vestibule which all must pass before they can enter the temple of wisdom.—When we are in doubt and puzzle out the truth by our own exertions we have gained something that will stay by us and will serve us again.—But if to avoid the trouble of the search we avail ourselves of the superior information of a friend, such knowledge will not remain with us; we have not bought, but borrowed it."

And Goethe sums it up with his statement, "Give me the benefit of your convictions, if you have any, but keep your doubts to yourself, for I have enough of my own." Don't spread your doubts; dominate them.

Crab grass grew in my yard when I first moved to South Florida. At that time I wanted any kind of grass to grow there—anything but sand. Later I killed the crab grass in order to grow beautiful St. Augustine grass. Similarly the doubts we have are temporary expediencies that help us move into the full palace room of power and achievement.

Gain self-confidence by dominating your doubts. Only a fool never has doubts, but a wise man never yields to them. He brings them rigidly under control. Be a dictator— over doubts, that is. Dominate them and you will be successful.

19. ACT AGGRESSIVELY

YOUR KEY for today is to act aggressively. Seize the day. Grapple with the hour. Assault the minute. To gain courage you must act aggressively. Remember our actions are our moods. Positive assertive action will drive away despondency.

In order to act you must first have confidence in yourself. You are better than you think you are. You can accomplish; but you must act—act now and act aggressively.

Why do you fail to act aggressively? Is it that you do not know your job? We are down on that with which we are unfamiliar.

Each year in America our economy loses billions of dollars because of insufficient, untrained, uninformed employees. An aggressive company will train its people. Now if you are not adequately trained for your task and there is no plan on the immediate horizon for training you, what should you do? The answer is train yourself. Read books on your field. Every field in America has some kind of training procedure and books that you can secure. Also read books on personality development.[1]

There is no excuse for becoming a failure. Act aggressively by learning and mastering your job. Then it becomes a joyous privilege and not a tedious task.

Go Upstream and Succeed

Let me urge you to do the opposite of the majority of people. A man without purpose is applying only about 30 per cent of his ability. If you do not have purpose, multiply your present salary by three and the figure you get is the one that you will be making if you apply your total ability, experience, knowledge and capacity by dynamic purpose. But you must violate the norm. Earl Nightingale says that only 5 per cent of American men are outstandingly successful. Dare to be different, and I believe you will find that you can be outstandingly successful.

In May, 1962, the stock market had a sudden drop. It was the most sustained paper loss since 1929. Frenzy and frustration swept the market. People called their brokers and yelled, "Sell." J. Paul Getty, one of the world's richest men, watched the situation very carefully and then ordered his brokers to buy. He bought at a low price. Within fifteen months the market was back ahead of where it was in May, 1962. Getty and others who bought at the low level became amazingly wealthy because they dared to be different. They went against the stream.

Paul J. Meyer, the million dollar personal success man, has the following dynamic points of success:[2]

"(1) Crystallize your thinking. Determine what specific goal you want to achieve and then dedicate yourself to its attainment with unswerving singleness of purpose.

"(2) Develop a plan for achieving your goal and a deadline for its attainment. Plan your progress carefully, hour by hour, day by day, month by month. Organize

---

[1]For instance, Dale Carnegie's *How To Win Friends and Influence People*, Gabriel's *Twenty Steps to Power and Influence and Control Over People*, and Battista's *The Power to Influence People*.
[2]From a conversation with Paul Meyer.

activity and maintain the enthusiasm of the well springs of your power.

"(3) Develop a sincere desire for the things you want in life. A burning desire is the greatest motivator of every human action. The desire for success implants success consciousness which in turn creates a vigorous and ever-increasing habit of success.

"(4) Develop supreme confidence in yourself and your own abilities. Enter every activity without giving mental recognition to the possibility of defeat. Concentrate on your strength instead of your weaknesses; on your powers instead of your problems.

"(5) Develop a dogged determination to follow through on your plan regardless of obstacles, criticisms or circumstances. Opportunities never come to those who wait, they are captured by those who dare to attack." Act aggressively.

Dress the Part

A practical way to overcome discouragement and to develop your action is the way that you dress. For example, wearing hard heels gives you a sense of purpose and achievement as you walk forcefully down the street. The clicking of the heels is an act of aggression and certainty.

Recently a friend of mine bought me a suit. When I have an important engagement or a speaking opportunity I wear that $175 suit. It does something to my mood. Self-confidence is destroyed in the presence of a person who is much more attractively dressed than yourself. Don't let this happen. You will find that a $100 or $125 suit will last twice as long as a $40 suit. And in all of the time you are wearing it, it will increase your effectiveness and efficiency by giving you self-confidence.

Ninety per cent of a man's body is covered by clothing. That leaves only his hands and face to be the "real person." Therefore clothing creates an important impression. Consult your tailor. Get a professional opinion. Don't wear the clothes that you like; wear the clothes that are best for you—that bring out your best. Wear the clothes that help you act aggressively. I love the story of the dynamic young man just out of college who applied for a position at a bank. The personnel officer asked him what he was capable of doing, and the young man replied that he wanted to be a vice-president. The personnel manager, quite shocked, said, "Why we already have twelve vice-presidents." The aggressive young man replied, "That's all right. I'm not superstitious."

Seize the day! Grab hold of life! Wrestle some opportunity! Get your share of success! Don't bog down in the quagmire of distrust, fear and frustration. By acting aggressively you can climb the mountaintop of glorious achievement. You can be successful.

20. POSSESS YOUR MIND

YOUR KEY to personal success is to control your mind and master your emotions. How many people do you know who really do *not* control their own minds? Some have yielded to others. Many have given their minds to habits of destruction—the alcoholics, dope addicts and pleasure-mad individuals who exist only for self-satisfaction.

True greatness is attained in service to others. So possess your mind. Do not be a victim going over the falls; be a victor climbing the rapids to achievement. "You have not only the power to think but, what is a thousand times more important still, you have the power to control your thoughts and to direct them to do your bidding. . . . You are the sum total of your dominating and most prominent thoughts," observed Napoleon Hill.

You change your manner and tone of voice to hide your true feelings from those you do not want to share them with. You control yourself because you want to. Now do the same with your mind. Master it. Control it. Make it serve you.

The Bible says, "As a man thinketh in his heart so is he." Our dominant thoughts make us what we are. In I Peter 1:13 we have these words: "Gird up the loins of your mind." Use your thoughts and control them.

Happiness Is a State of Mind

Everyone wants to be happy. But happiness is not a goal; it is a state of mind. "A merry heart doeth good like a medicine: but a broken spirit drieth the bones" (Proverbs 17:22).

An old Dutch proverb says, "Happy people are never wicked." You can do something about being happy. Abraham Lincoln said, "Most people are about as happy as they make up their minds to be."

Drive away the dregs and disease of despair. Determine you are going to be happy.

Napoleon Hill lists the following twelve great riches of life: "(1) A positive mental attitude. (2) Sound physical health. (3) Harmony in human relationships. (4) Freedom from fear. (5) Hope of achievement. (6) The capacity for faith. (7) Willingness to share one's blessings. (8) A labor of love. (9) An open mind on all subjects. (10) Self-discipline. (11) The capacity to understand people. (12) Financial security."[1]

These are certainly worthy goals for all men to attain but, remember, there is nothing in all this world that you influence more than your own mind. In Romans 6:16 we have these words: "Know ye not, that to whom ye yield yourselves servants to obey, his servants ye are to whom ye obey; whether of sin unto death, or of obedience unto righteousness?" Look again. Either our minds are mastered by our wills and become servants to our goals of success or our minds can be enslaved to destructive habits, to corrosive conduct and to ruinous deeds.

Life is for living. Life is for attainment. "Possess your mind and you will have confidence."

Build Confidence and Succeed

A confident, continuous, positive attitude assures you of a habit of succeeding:

1. State your purpose with bolder confidence than you have previously.

2. You can whip worry with enthusiastic action. Outline your action.

    A.

    B.

    C.

    D.

---

[1]Napoleon Hill, *The Master Key to Riches* (Los Angeles: Willing Publishing Company, 1945), pages 29-34.

3. You can fight fear with facts:

Fact 1. You're a free man in a free society.
Fact 2. You have increasing desire to excel.
Fact 3. You can find the solution to any problem.
Fact 4. You now have a purpose greater than yourself.
Fact 5. You are among the top 5 per cent in the nation.
(Fill in the others yourself.)
Fact 6.
Fact 7.
Fact 8.

4. You can dominate and dictate your doubts:

A. Who's greater, the unlimited you or that negative emotion Doubt?

B. Aggressive action will destroy doubt. Describe your immediate action.

C. Improve your wardrobe and lift your moods. What clothes do you need now?

5. You can possess and empower your mind. List the constructive ways you will reconstruct your positive mind.

A.

B.

C.

PART FIVE
THE POWER OF PERSISTENCE

21. PERSISTENCE PRODUCES POWER

YOUR KEY for personal success is persistence, for persistence produces power. Let me tell you the story about one of America's most outstanding failures. In 1831 he failed in business. In 1832 he was defeated for the Legislature. In 1833 he again failed in business. In 1834 he was elected to the Legislature. In 1838 he was defeated for Speaker; in 1840 defeated for Elector; in 1843 defeated for Congress; in 1846 elected to Congress; in 1848 defeated for Congress; in 1855 defeated for Senate; in 1856 defeated for Vice-President; in 1858 defeated for Senate; in 1860 elected to President of the United States.

His name? Abraham Lincoln. Who else could have been able to bear the adversity that Lincoln bore during those tragic days of the Civil War? Nearly half of his cabinet was opposed to him. When asked why he didn't fire them he said, "Don't I rid myself of my enemies by making them my friends?" At his death they all stood and honored him with total loyalty. He was able to hold the Northern states together by the power of his dedication and conviction, and he saved the Union by the force of that conviction. Yet in the process he destroyed one of America's greatest blights—slavery.

Lincoln learned persistence by being victor over many adversities in the formative years of his life. The proving ground of greatness is how we bounce back from life's troubles and tribulations. Persistence is the power that produces amazing achievement. Bacon has said, "Great efforts come of industry and perseverance; for audacity doth almost bind and mate the weaker sort of minds."

Learn from Every Disappointment

After one particularly happy vocational experience of several years a friend said, "You know, you've had it so good. Things have gone so easy and so well with so little opposition that one of these days you may find yourself in hot water because you haven't, by necessity, had to learn how to deal with problems, opposition and difficulties."

Since there is no substitute for personal experience, my friend had a point. My answer that many people cause their own problems by failing to count the cost, failing to consider all of the facts and then starting off half cocked before they gain the fellowship of the people involved, was a halfhearted reply. The truth of his statement had driven home. The man who has had to pick himself up from the disappointments and difficulties of life has learned a valuable lesson. Nothing deters him. Nothing frustrates him. Nothing upsets him. He has traveled that course before and he knows the answer. And he is persistent.

Never forget the words of Marshall Foch, the French Commander in World War I, when the battlefield situation was as tragic as could be: "My center is giving way, my right is pushed back, situation excellent, I am attacking"

"Perseverance gives power to weakness, and opens to poverty the world's wealth. It spreads fertility over the barren landscape, and bids the choicest fruits and flowers spring up and flourish in the desert abode of thorns and briers." —S. G. Goodrich.

How to Be a Genius

How prone we are to write off the outstanding achievement of another person by saying, "Well, he's a genius," "Look at his opportunities," "Look at his education," or some such trite statement. Never forget Thomas A. Edison's remark, "Achievement is 2 per cent inspiration and 98 per cent perspiration." What is a genius? Genius is the power of making continuous effort. You don't even know when you've approached or you've crossed the line of failure and success, it is so fine. But I'll tell you when you've crossed it—when you continue to persistently pursue your goal—when you let nothing deter you nor detour you—when your purpose pulsates and your goal guides and your motivation challenges and inspires—then that's genius.

On March 15, 1915, the British Navy attacked the Turks at the Dardanelles. There was a terrific Naval barrage from the guns on the shore. Three ships had been sunk and finally, just at noon, the British Navy withdrew never to take that point during that engagement. What they didn't know was that the Turks had only sixty seconds of ammunition left and at that very moment were preparing to surrender. Had the British Navy been persistent and continued to press the battle they would have taken the Dardanelles, split the enemy forces, closed the war years earlier and saved millions of lives. Oh, the tragedy of failing to persevere.

The Turtle Won the Prize

Remember that childhood story of the hare and the turtle? The most promising boy in my high school class is today, at forty, a hopeless alcoholic. He was the hare—a big spurt and then a good time. Hang the goal. But there was another boy, picked on, poked fun at, limited in athletic ability (never did letter, just went out for the basketball team) but continuously at it. Where is he at forty? An amazingly successful insurance executive—a millionaire. He was persistent.

Pathway in Your Brain

The subconscious mind never argues. It takes orders and never rests. Therefore the conscious mind must consistently and persistently command the subconscious mind to bring forth the results of its ceaseless labor. Thus we are building a conditioned consciousness, a habitual feeling or a habitual condition by which we achieve. Remember, "As a man thinketh in his heart so is he." We become what we think about. The persistent command drives a pathway, a channel, a canal, a ditch, a roadway through the impressions of our mind and brings forth the desired result.

One study in business found that 80 per cent of the sales were made after the fifth call. Forty-eight per cent of the salesmen quit after the first call, 25 per cent quit after the second call, 12 per cent quit after the third call, 10 per cent of the salesmen keep calling and make 80 per cent of the sales. Persistence pays off. Persistence provides power. Do you want it? It's up to you. Do you realize how bored some people are the second and third time they hear anything? How do we learn? By repetition. What's the principle of advertising? Repeating the same story over and over and over. For example: How many settlers were killed by the Indians west of the Mississippi River? Only thirty-six. But from reading all of the stories and seeing all the movies and TV extravaganzas of the Indian uprisings in the West you would think that millions of Americans had been slaughtered by the Indians. You see the story has been told so long and so often, with so much impact and color, that we believe the Red River actually was named that because its banks flowed with the blood of the settlers. Repetition makes impact. So be persistent and you will accomplish.

Repeat and Reap Results

In his book, *How I Discovered the Secret of Success in the Bible,* Davidson says, "What makes repetition so powerful a factor in effective suggestion? What purpose does it serve? (1) The human mind cannot act on what it does not understand. Repetition, especially when it presents a proposition in many ways, serves to make the idea clearer. (2) Repetition wears down the resisting power of those contrary ideas which entangle your idea or suggestion and prevent its ready acceptance by your prospect's mind."[1]

Let me quote you that tremendous statement by Irving Black on this principle: "No doubt a good many of us have seen a pile driving machine at its work. Poised in mid-air is the weight of the driving part of the machine. Suddenly this weight of several tons is let loose. . . . We would think that the log would be driven down its whole length with this terrific impact but it is hardly moved a fraction of an inch. Again that same terrific impact and again there is that slight embedment in the ground. And so on this process continues for weeks until the proper foundation is made. It is this cumulative process, this constant hammering, this continuous driving force, that finally erects a foundation upon which to build a permanent structure. It is this same law, this cumulative law, that causes men of obscurity to become famous. It is this steadiness of purpose that lifts men out of the chaos of poverty into the heights of prosperity. It is this sincerity of accomplishment that differentiates between the doer and the wisher."[2]

Pile Drive Your Way to Success

Pick out your foundation, drive your stake in it and start pile driving, hour after hour, day after day, impact upon impact. You can achieve through persistence. There is no other emotion, no other thing that is as powerful as persistence. You can have anything you want if you will pay the price of persistence, staying after the effort. Let

---

[1] Davidson, *Ibid.*, pages 79-80.
[2] Davidson, *Ibid.*, page 81.

your goal be, "Day by day I'm on my way." Say it over and over again and you will succeed.

Great Men Work

"Though you may have known clever men who were indolent, you never knew a great man who was so; and when I hear a young man spoken of as giving promise of great genius, the first question I ask about him always is, does he work?"—John Ruskin.

Dr. David Seabury, the psychologist said, "One could not overstate what attention refocused could do for a person if consistently, insistently, incessantly and persistently carried out. No aberration could remain in control of anyone if this process was earnestly fulfilled. Nor would the supposed external barriers to success, health and happiness, long remain as obstacles. Every negative has its positive, every loss a potential gain, every evil a hidden good. Such a statement is not mere optimism but the simple provable truth. To turn attention to finding and using the good with which to overcome the evil is one of the greatest secrets of true living. From doing so we will give our human attention a natural basis for fulness and power."

Engineers have proven that troops in cadence cannot cross a bridge. It will break if they try. Well do I remember in the military how, when we approached a bridge, we would fall out of step and walk across careful not to be in cadence. Yes, repetition is one of the most powerful forces in the world. You can be successful through persistence. I challenge you to do so today.

22. PERSISTENCE EMPOWERS PURPOSE

YOUR KEY for personal success today is persistence, and persistence empowers dynamic purpose. You can be successful.

What is the first response that comes to your heart when you are faced with a problem? That's right—to quit, to give up. A boy was burned so horribly that his legs were expected to be amputated, but he didn't give up. They said that he wouldn't walk again but he did. He made a pathway, holding onto the picket fence. He disciplined himself in steel will. He paid the price in fantastic persistence. As a result he became one of the world's greatest distance runners. His name—Glenn Cunningham. He discovered that persistence empowers purpose.

If you are persistent long enough, you too will determine and develop amazing purpose.

Your Job and Long Life

John E. Gibson, in a news article entitled *Science Looks at Your Job*, reports that your profession actually affects the length of your life. For example, educators and lawyers, two groups that have to pay the most persistent price in achieving their service in life, live longest. Next came scientific and engineering pursuits, third were philosophical and theological callings. Doctors ranked next. Then painters and musicians, followed by writers and actors. Explorers and poets averaged the shortest life span. Furthermore this study showed that the individuals who achieved the greatest distinction in their professions averaged much longer life spans than the less eminent.

These same professions rate the highest in prestige as well. For instance, doctors have the highest prestige rating in the minds of most people, with college professors, scientists and bankers running a very close second. An army psychologist found that professions averaging the highest intelligence scores were accounting, engineering, medicine and chemistry. Occupations ranking next highest in the I.Q. department included writers, educators, lawyers and dentists. "In a wide scale study conducted by the University of Minnesota Investigators it was found that the persons whose occupations made continuous demands on their intelligence, mental ability, tended to increase more definitely with age. Furthermore, many people of high achievement do not have above average I.Q.s but the quality most successful men *do have* in common is persistence and the capacity to make fullest use of their abilities."[1]

The reason these professions rank so high in achievement, in long life and in prestige is that these men were persistently after their purpose in life. And as their persist-

---

[1]*Our Changing World*, No. 641.

ence empowered their purpose, their purpose was a motivating factor to develop persistence. You cannot have one without the other.

Recently there has been talk about men with super-bodies, that is men who work long and strenuous hours under tremendous pressure. Some of these men have found that health problems developed—a heart condition—and they were forced to take a rest period. One study showed that while these men were recuperating from a heart condition, even when they were supposed to be resting, they actually had established another business. Do they really have super-bodies? No. Actually they have super-purpose and powerful persistence.

Control Your Length of Life

You may ask, "Are you suggesting that people can actually control the length of their life?" Yes, I most emphatically am. Medical science agrees that the most important factor in any illness is the will to live. On a number of occasions I've seen people get well by the sheer persistence and determination to do so. And I've seen other people die simply because they felt they didn't have anything to live for. The man who is persistently serving a worthy purpose will care for himself. He will take care of his body. He will see that the necessities and needs are met—that adequate recreation is a part of the routine of his life. Furthermore the man who persistently is empowered to achieve a worthy purpose (for we've said that the science of success is the persistent achievement of a challenging worthy goal) is not as prone to be fraught with worry and frustration and hyper-tension. You see, he's beyond himself. He is not constantly looking inward at his own personal problems.

Be Failure-Proof

To be failure-proof you must have an unconquerable faith, totally consistent and goal-directed emotions, a will surrendered to a cause greater than yourself, and an idea for achievement or service that has incubated its time and is now ready to hatch into acceptability.

Be the Master of Your Moods

One of the great powers of developing persistent purpose is to control our moods. Thanks to the recently developed field of Business Men's Records there is available for you today a planned program to develop persistent purpose. Paul J. Meyer, president of Success Motivation Institute of Waco, Texas, and other firms, have a number of outstanding recordings that you can use to cultivate your purpose. I purchased a transistorized record player that I can take in my brief case along with several records. Then in a hotel room, or in an office waiting for a conference, or whatever the circumstance, I can cultivate and develop my persistence. Never let those moments be wasted.

Change Possibilities to Probabilities

First, you must be upset with discontent. Inventor Charles Kettering said, "A problem well stated is half solved." Then, second, you must vividly imagine the long-range goal. Third, you should build excitement by listing all the benefits to yourself, your family, and to everyone involved. Fourth, you must dedicate yourself, commit yourself, surrender yourself, to the attainment of this goal.

The achievement of your goal is assured the moment you commit yourself to it. The realization will require time.

Imagination dreams, goals direct, enthusiasm propels, and persistence produces.

God Give Us Men

The decision is yours. Will you pay the price of persistent effort—never giving up, never wavering, never swerving from your purpose—always staying at it? You will succeed. Martin Luther changed the whole course of theological history. Remember his words, "It is neither safe nor prudent to do aught against conscience. Here I stand— I can do no otherwise. God help me. Amen."

God give us men! A time like this demands
Strong minds, great hearts, true faith and ready hands;
Men whom the lust of office does not kill;
Men whom the spoils of office cannot buy;
Men who possess opinions and a will;
Men who have honor; men who will not lie;
Men who can stand before a demagogue
And damn his treacherous flatteries without winking!

Tall men, sun-crowned, who live above the fog
In public duty and in private thinking;
For while the rabble, with their thumb-worn creeds,
Their large professions and their little deeds,
Mingle in selfish strife, lo! Freedom weeps,
Wrong rules the land and waiting Justice sleeps.

—J. G. Holland

No Man Is an Island

We become what the people we associate with are.
Therefore your persistence in achieving a worthy purpose
will be a part of the total triumph of good, the total
triumph of democracy, the total triumph of all that's
wholesome in your society. At the same time laziness is
cancerous; it is catching. One person who has found that
he can get by on the unemployed rolls is a challenge to
others to do the same. All you have to do to fail is to do
nothing. That's it. Simply drift downstream with the tide.
But there is no power, no muscles, no strength, no character involved in that fatal activity. There is strength and
character and power energized when we fight the stream,
particularly when it is mountainous, turbulent, hard to go
upstream.

Bogardus's book *Leaders and Leadership*[2] has meant
more to my life than possibly any other book except the
Bible. In it Borgardus quotes Admiral Dewey, "Perhaps
some boy may have since excelled me in the length of
time that he could hold his head under water but my
record was unbeaten in my day."

John Wesley, who traveled on horseback over land and
by slow sail ship at sea, traveled a total of 250,000 miles
in his lifetime, preaching as often as fifteen times a day
throughout fifty years. "He had read books while making
his horseback journeys and yet, when past eighty he com-
plains that he cannot read and work more than fifteen
hours a day." The doctors told him that he would have to
slow down. He did—by only preaching eight times a day.
Of Charlemagne, Bogardus said, "He was so hardy, they
tell us, that he would hunt the wild bull singlehanded, so
strong that he felled a horse and rider with one blow. Add
to these external traits a tireless energy, an iron will, a

---

[2]Emory S. Bogardus, *Leaders and Leadership* (New York:
Appleton-Century-Crofts, Inc., 1934), page 298.

keen love of order and of justice, deep-seated religious instincts and under all an exuberant animal nature; such is the man as he appeared to his contemporaries."

When Thomas A. Edison was working on the phonograph he had difficulty reproducing the letter S. He would work eighteen and twenty hours a day for weeks and weeks at a time before he came up with the solution. He would not quit.

Booker T. Washington said, "I have begun everything with the idea that I could succeed."

The Priest Who Persevered

Francisco Palou, in his book *The Life of Junipero Serra,* tells of the persistence of this Catholic priest to reach his work in the west: "When the Governor saw what a plight he was in he said; 'Your reverend well knows that you cannot accompany the expedition. We are only six leagues from the place from which we set out. If your reverend will permit they will carry you back to the first mission in order that you there become well again and we will go on with our journey.' But our venerable father, who will never give up, replied in this manner; 'Please do not speak to me further about the matter because I trust in God who will give me strength to arrive at San Diego, if He's given me strength to come this far, and in case this is not His good pleasure for me, I shall resign myself to His holy will. Even if I die on the road I will not go back, but you can bury me here, and I shall very gladly remain among these pagan people if such be the will of God for me.' "[3]

Persistence and purpose provide tremendous courage. Lyman Abbott in his book *Henry Ward Beecher* tells the following incident: "In Elizabeth City, New Jersey, Beecher was to address a crowd of ruffians who declared that they would kill him if he attempted to speak there. Surrounded by a loyal band he was ushered into the hall and to the platform. As he began to speak he said: 'Gentlemen, I have been informed that if I attempted to speak tonight I am to be killed. Well I am going to speak and therefore I must die. But before you kill me there is one

[3]Francisco Palou, *The Life of Junipero Serra* (Pasadena, Calif.: George W. James, 1913), page 71.

request that I am going to make. All you who are to stain your hands with my blood just come up here and shake hands with me before you commit the crime for when I die I shall go to heaven and therefore I shall not see any of you again.' "[4] They heard him out. Who could stand against such courage and persistence?

Courage Overcomes the Coward

When Samuel Gompers was presiding over a heated meeting of the American Federation of Labor held in Albany, New York, he was rushed upon and attacked. "John Brophy rushed from the rear of the room, scaled the bar and jumped upon the platform where I was standing. He pointed a revolver in my breast. It was certainly a startling scene. I did not touch the revolver or make any attempt to touch his hand but with my left hand I caught the lapel of his coat and extended my right palm forward and in as emphatic a tone as I could command, said: 'Give me that pistol.' He did not give it to me and still louder and with all the emphasis I could command I repeated my demand. At the third repetition he dropped the pistol into my hand and then bedlam broke loose. I then protected him from them."[5]

Gompers was dedicated to his beliefs of labor. Persistence had developed purpose and courage. He would not be deterred.

You can build a tower of fantastic success but you must first draw in your mind's eye the architectural sketches. Then you must lay a brick every day. If you lay a brick a day or several a day and everlastingly stay at it, your castle will be built, your tower will be achieved and you will stand there for all to see and respect as long as you live and, yea, much longer even than that.

The decision is yours. You can be successful but you must pay the price of persistence, for persistence empowers purpose. You cannot continue to do any one thing with persistence without developing amazing purpose in the process.

---

[4]Lyman Abbott, *Henry Ward Beecher* (Boston: Houghton-Mifflin Company, 1903), page 316.
[5]Samuel Gompers, *Seventy Years of Life and Labor* (New York: E. P. Dutton and Company, Inc., 1925), page 277.

The Power of Persistence

Persistent action produces the power and the habit of succeeding:

1. Restate your major purpose. Now add the persistent action necessary for its achievement.

2. How will you cultivate the habit of this persistent action?

3. Genius is the power of making continuous effort. What are the five benefits you will enjoy once you have attained your purpose?

    A.
    B.
    C.
    D.
    E.

4. To the 95 per cent who fail you will be a genius. State the reasons you have failed to be persistent in the past.

    A.
    B.
    C.

State how you will overcome each.

    A.
    B.
    C.

23. PERSISTENCE PAYS HIGH PROFITS

YOUR KEY for personal success for today is persistence. You can be successful by paying the price of persistence. Persistence produces peace. Let's take two men. One is aimless, no purpose, no direction, no goal. He is a hobo if he is broke; he is a playboy if he has inherited a fortune. Is he happy? You tell me.

Now let's take the second man. He is persistently achieving a worthy, challenging goal, whether it's the milkman who delivers this important item to your front door or the corporation lawyer. He knows where he is going. He has the joy of achievement. He brings his pay check home weekly or monthly with a sense of accomplishment. He returns a certain portion of it to the religious and benevolent needs of his community. He invests at least 10 per cent of it as a safeguard against rainy days and old age. He is meeting the obligations of his family. Now tell me which man is at peace?

Yes, persistence produces peace and contentment in a man's heart. Real peace comes when we are using our abilities, our powers, our God-given talents for the achievement of a worthy goal. The more purposeful, the busier an individual, the happier he is. Dean Briggs[1] emphasized this: "Do your work. Not just your work and no more, but a little more for the lavishing sake, that little more which is worth all the rest. And if you doubt as you must; and if you suffer as you must—do your work. Put your heart into it and the sky will clear. Then out of your very doubt and suffering will be born the supreme joy of life."

The mother whose primary goal in life is to send her children forth in maturity as outstanding citizens of the land, who is joyfully contented with the efforts of giving these children the best that she can in character training

---

[1]Dean LeBaron Russell Briggs of Harvard and later President of Radcliffe.

and in personal guidance will not be neurotic. Her purpose demands persistence, and her persistent efforts day by day produce joy and peace in her heart.

A Motto to Make Your Work Joyful

How do you like your job? Do you get up in the morning eager to go to work? Do you have difficulty leaving your work in the afternoon to go home to your family and civic and church responsibilities? Do you enjoy taking your work home with you, not out of necessity but out of the vibrant joy of achievement? Do you find yourself having difficulty crowding in a vacation and the day off? I'm not suggesting that you become a work addict as some have become because they are neurotically involved. But do you work for the sheer joy of it? Do you like your job?

Recent studies have revealed that a lot of people, in fact the majority of people, do not like their jobs but when asked the question, "What would you like to do?" they have no answer. Notice the negativism of it: not happy where they are but not knowing where they want to go—no joy, no peace, because no persistence. They are living for a dollar rather than for a purpose.

Let one of your mottoes be, "The greatest use of life is to so use your life that the use of your life will outlive your life." Find a purpose beyond yourself and persistently bring all of your talents, ability, mind power, personality to bear upon achieving that goal. You will have peace in your heart and you will be able to sleep comfortably at night. Louis Kossuth has said, "The palm-tree grows best beneath a ponderous weight, and even so the character of man. ... The petty pangs of small daily cares have often bent the character of men, but great misfortunes seldom."

The Harder the Training the Better the Product

The burden of a great and glorious responsibility involving a dynamic purpose that you are persistently pursuing doesn't break your back, nor does the load of it bring abulia or a nervous breakdown. I have observed Coach Frank Broyles, now at the University of Arkansas, in training his team, bringing them to the peak of physical perfection and timing and team play as they exact to a science the laws of football achievement. His record in the Southwest Conference, year after year being champion or co-champion, is proof that the finer the training the better the product. Persistence brings peace in the achievement and satisfaction of arriving at the goal. Coach Bud Wilkinson, then at the University of Oklahoma, had his players climb, in tennis shoes, the stadium steps from the playing field all the way to the top, bringing their physical facilities to the height of perfection. His teams through the years have proven the importance of persistence, and there is peace in being a member of a championship organization.

Those of us in the ranks didn't understand what was being done during those agonizing months of strenuous training in 1944 and 1945 as our division was being honed to a peak of military perfection, through the jungles and on the beaches, fording the rivers and climbing the mountainous ranges on Guadalcanal in preparation for the invasion of Okinawa. However our Divisional Commander, Major General Lenuel C. Shephard, Jr., knew what he was doing and the Sixth Marine Division received the Presidential Unit Citation because he led us in persistently paying the price of purpose. Peace was the result. We are talking about the personal peace of individual achievement that comes in a man's heart when he knows he has done his best, and that best is a part of all the good that's round about him everywhere.

Persistence Provides a Bride

Did you hear about the young man who was in love with a young lady but his company transferred him out of town for a year? He knew that persistence paid off so he decided he would hold her attention by mailing her a postcard every day for a year, and he did. At the end of the year she married—the postman. Now the persistence of that daily visit by the postman brought him to the attention of the young lady. She couldn't resist such persistence.

Hugh Blair has said, "Industry is not only the instrument of improvement but the foundation of pleasure.... He who is a stranger to it may possess, but cannot enjoy, for it is labor only which gives relish to pleasure.... It is the indispensable condition of possessing a sound mind in a sound body, and is the appointed vehicle of every good to man." You see, joy hovers about the head of the man who loves his own occupation.

In the Bible, Job 11:15-19 (ASV) says, "Yea, thou shalt be stedfast, and shalt not fear: For thou shalt forget thy misery; Thou shalt remember it as waters that are passed away. And thy life shall be clearer than the noonday; Though there be darkness, it shall be as the morning. And thou shalt be secure, because there is hope; Yea, thou shalt search about thee, and shalt take thy rest in safety. Also thou shalt lie down, and none shall make thee afraid."

Remember those times when you started a task and then stopped in the middle of it? You let something else divert your attention or you simply did not pay the self-discipline of completion. Not only were you embarrassed when associates called for the information and you didn't have it; not only were you hurt when you passed the deadline and your work and others suffered; but you lost self-respect—you didn't complete your job. Never forget that what you think about yourself is merely an opinion of what others think about you, for others' attitudes reflect themselves in our outlook, our moods constantly. If others are appreciative of our efforts, our work, and our presence, this reflects itself in our personal outlook. Certainly if they are negative toward us we will be negative in turn. So gain this peace of self-achievement by persisting and you will be successful.

Your Eight-Point Pathway to Success

In his book *How To Turn Failure Into Success* Harold Sherman has given the code of persistence. Let me quote it for you: "(1) I will never give up so long as I know I am right. (2) I will believe that all things will work out for me if I hang on to the end. (3) I will be courageous and undismayed in the face of odds. (4) I will not permit anyone to intimidate me or deter me from my goal. (5) I will fight to overcome all physical handicaps and setbacks. (6) I will try again and again and yet again to accomplish what I desire. (7) I will take new faith and resolution from the knowledge that all successful men and women have had to fight defeat and adversity. (8) I will never surrender to discouragement or despair no matter what seeming obstacles may confront me."[1]

John Ruskin has said, "God intends no man to live in this world without working; but it seems to me no less evident that he intends every man to be happy in his work." Calvin Coolidge said, "Nothing in the world can take the place of persistence. Talent will not; nothing is more common than unsuccessful men with talent. Genius will not; unrewarded genius is almost a proverb. Education will not; the world is full of educated derelicts. Persistence and determination alone are omnipotent. The slogan 'Press on' has solved and always will solve the problems of the human race."

It is all up to you. You can be successful. You can have peace in your heart and look at every day with joy and purpose. You can come to the end of life's journey with fulfillment and achievement and hosts of friends who pay you the praise for a life wonderfully and richly invested and productive. I challenge you to find a purpose; pursue that purpose with persistence and you will have peace in your own heart.

24. PERSISTENCE IS EDUCATION

YOUR KEY for personal success is to accomplish endurance through persistence. The word persistent means to persevere, tenacious. Tenacious means adhesive, determined.

Clarence Day in his book *Life With Father* suggests the power of persistence with the following statement: "Father declared he was going to buy a new plot in the cemetery, a plot all for himself. 'And I will buy one on a corner,' he added triumphantly, 'where I can get out.' Mother looked at him, startled but admiringly, and whispered to me, 'I almost believe he could do it.' "[2] Here's a statement of a man so persistent in his daily pursuits that

---

[1]Sherman, *Ibid.*, page 138.
[2]Clarence Day, *Life With Father*, (New York: Knopf, 1935).

his loved ones actually expected him to be effective in eternity.

Have you ever gotten to that place in your life when you wondered if it were worth it all? When you've been striving so hard and the answers have not yet come? You were just about ready to quit. But do you remember the occasion when you pressed on just a little bit more and suddenly everything fit into place? You were amazed to find the answer so close, the light of morning so near. Remember the darkest is just before the dawn.

Max Otto has written a statement that pertains here: "Along the upper reaches of the Ohio where the foothills of the Allegheny mountains hem in one of America's beautiful streams you sometimes awake at daybreak to find that a heavy mist has obliterated the landscape leaving only a narrow circle of it dimly visible about you. When this happens you resign yourself to the weather and wait for a change or you may do what you have on hand with the best cheer you can muster, calling to the neighbor whose shadowy form you can see though you cannot be sure what he is doing. If you keep busy the mist rises. You see the river rolling on toward the Mississippi. Then you see the opposite shore, the houses of the city, the taller buildings, the towers of the schools, the steeples of the churches highest of all. Slowly the mist climbs the hills, hangs for a little like a torn veil on the summit, then vanishes, disclosing a blue sky. And the work you began in the fog you continue in the sunlight."[2]

Court Three Ladies at Once

Enduring a little bit longer may bring fabulous inroads of achievement pouring out upon you far beyond your fondest imagination. The world belongs to him who patiently perseveres. It is yours. It is waiting for you to attain it. But, remember, fortune and fame and success—all of these are fickle ladies that have to be pursued. Like the proverbial old maid—they want to be wed but they want to be sure they are wanted. They have some question marks about the sincerity of your purpose. They have seen other friends hurt down through the years, so these three are waiting for you to prove yourself. If you endure,

[2]*Our Changing World*, No. 574.

persevere, persist, you soon will have their hand. It's up to you.

Opportunity always comes disguised as hard work but God never shuts one door but He opens another. Life's great opportunities often open on the road of daily duties. You must keep enduring, day after day, never turning back, and you will be successful.

Work Is Love Made Visible

In *The Prophet* Kahlil Gibran wrote, "Work is love made visible. And if you cannot work with love but only with distaste, it is better that you should leave your work and sit at the gate of the temple and take alms of those who work with joy."

"Work is love made visible." Remember mother's love expressed in so many wondrous ways? Remember the days of the depression—how limiting they were? My father was pastor of a church in a small town. He had been there three years and they were one year behind in his salary and they only paid him $100 a month. How the love of my parents showed itself in so many wondrous ways. Work is love in action.

The home is a haven and a heaven on earth, a refuge from man's most difficult hours at work. A man can take anything at work if there is joy and happiness and peace at home. A man can accomplish much more at work if he feels his work is love made visible, that he is doing it because it is an expression of his love to his children and to his wife, and perhaps to his aged parents. You can endure and in endurance there is success.

Education Sets Income

Persistence pays off in so many wondrous ways. Do you realize that a high school graduate will earn $50,000 more in his lifetime than a man who quits before graduation? This means that every day a youngster stays in high school is worth $70 to him. And, of course, a college education is worth approximately $150,000 more in a man's lifetime than a person with an eighth grade education. The persistence of those formative years pays off tremendously in all of life's effectiveness.

Endurance is success. Goethe said, "He who moves not forward goes backward." Nothing stands still. Time isn't waiting for you to decide what you are going to do. Therefore, endure, persist, persevere, stay with it, pursue it.

Is there anything worse than self-doubt, self-pity, self-condemnation. This destroys endurance and persistence. Hillyer has written, "Self-doubt is caused by the fact that every human activity involves some other person whose praise or blame seems unduly important. We set a goal of perfection before ourselves and groaningly conclude that it cannot be achieved. But perfectionism is a dangerous state of mind in an imperfect world. The best way is to forget doubts and set about the task at hand. While the battle is being fought or the cake is baking in the oven, leave the outcome to the future where it belongs. If you are doing your best you will not have time to worry about failure."[3]

Who is calling the signals of your life? Remember what I said earlier—that your mind is the only thing in this world that you hold total control over. Now master it. Don't submit your mind, God-given and fantastic in its possibilities, to any other human. Keep your mind as the power of your own achievement. Therefore don't let others' criticisms, or doubts, or questions, or cynical rantings affect you. Determine what you are going to do. Let nothing in this world keep you from accomplishing it. Persist every day; endure, and you will achieve.

25. PERSISTENCE PRODUCES RESULTS

YOUR KEY for personal success is persistence because persistence produces results. You can be successful.

Recently in the Montgomery, Alabama, airport I met a successful businessman, a Mr. Smith from Atlanta. The friend who introduced us told me about Mr. Smith's tremendous success in his wholesale auto parts business. Upon congratulating him he answered, "Oh, I've been lucky." But success is not luck. Success can be predicted:

---

[3]*Our Changing World,* No. 788.

it can be assured. I asked further about Mr. Smith and here's the story:

Auto parts dealers found they were having difficulty getting parts. Supplies were arriving too slow so Mr. Smith suggested to his associates that he open up a clearing house in Atlanta. He assured them that for 2 per cent of the volume above cost he would set up a clearing house that would guarantee them their parts much more readily, quicker—far greater service than they were then having. They all agreed to enter into the covenant. In 1962 that warehouse did $10,000,000 of business. Now you figure what 2 per cent of that is. In 1963 they are expecting to do $13,000,000 of business. Luck? No, it is not luck. Mr. Smith had an idea and he persistently pursued that idea. Today the results are there as a reward, as a crowning achievement of persistently pursuing a worthy idea.

In Matthew 7:7 we read: "Keep on asking and the gift will be given you; keep on seeking, and you will find; keep on knocking and the door will open to you. For everyone who keeps on asking, receives, and everyone who keeps on seeking, finds, and to the one who keeps on knocking, the door will open."[1] That's it. If you keep on working, keep on asking, keep on seeking you inevitably will reach your goal.

There's No Such Thing As Luck

Some people destroy initiative by their attitude toward luck which can be as futilely fatalistic as *"Allah wills it."* Abe Lincoln had terribly bad luck in elections but persistence produced the Presidency. We should learn more from our defeats, by examining them more carefully, than we do from our victories. I've found in reading about hundreds of individuals, in personally observing dozens of friends, and in my personal experience that the harder one works the luckier one becomes.

Persistence Produced the Pontiac

At the outbreak of World War II, Doug Lewis, now Dean of Men at Hannibal-LaGrange College at Hannibal,

---

[1]Charles B. Williams, *The New Testament in the Language of the People* (Chicago: Moody Press, 1937).

Missouri, had a new Oldsmobile convertible. A personal friend of his, a Pontiac dealer in a small town in Missouri, wanted to buy the car. He entered into this covenant: if Doug would turn the car over to him then this Pontiac dealer assured Doug that the first car he received at the end of the war Doug Lewis would have. Remember how difficult it was to get cars those days, how few came off the assembly lines? Doug waited weeks and then found out that one car had been delivered to his friend, some hundred or more miles away from where he was living. He called him long distance and said, "I'm ready for my car." The man began to stumble and said, "Now wait. I promised you the first car after my wife got one, my salesmanager, my service manager, a demonstrator. You will have the first one I have for sale. I've got to supply my stock first." Doug didn't argue with him. He simply took a bus, arrived in the small town on Thursday after-noon, went down to the Pontiac dealer's office, greeted him, sat around and talked to him. It came time to close up. The dealer said, "Come on up to the house and have supper." And Doug did. He brought his bag along. After the supper they sat around talking. Then the dealer said, "Spend the night." Doug said, "I'll be happy to."

The next morning they had breakfast. Doug followed him down to the shop. All day he hung around. Went home with him that night. Spent the night. The next day, followed him around all day. Didn't say a word about the automobile. Saturday night Doug spent the night. Sunday he went to church. He stayed with the dealer all Sunday afternoon and Sunday night. On Monday he went to the office with him. Finally on Tuesday morning the dealer took the keys out of his pocket, threw them in Doug's lap and said, "Take it. You've worn me out." That's persist-ence. Results come to him who will persevere. It's up to you.

Think Big

In his book *The Magic of Thinking Big*, Schwartz has said, "(1) Believe it can be done. Believing a solution paves the way to solution. (2) Don't let tradition paralyze your mind. Be receptive to new ideas. Try new ap-proaches. Be progressive in everything you do. (3) Ask yourself daily, 'How can I do better? How can I be better?' (4) Ask yourself, 'How can I do more?' Capacity is a state of mind. (5) Practice asking and listening. Ask and listen and you will obtain raw material for reaching sound decisions. Remember big people monopolize the listening; small people monopolize the talking. (6) Stretch your mind. Get stimulated. Associate with people who can help you to think of new ideas, new ways of doing things and forever persevere."[2]

After a beautiful concert a lady rushed up to the pianist and gushed, "I'd give *anything* to play as you do." When the pianist replied, "Oh, no, you wouldn't," a hush fell over the group. Trying again the lady said, "I would too give anything to play the piano as you do." "No you wouldn't, if you would you could play as well, possibly a little better, than I do. You would give anything to play as I do except time, except the one thing it takes to accomplish the task. You wouldn't sit and practice hour after hour, day after day, year after year." Then she flashed a warm smile. "Understand," she said, "I'm not criticizing you. I'm just telling you that when you say you would give anything to play as I do you really don't mean it."

You can have most anything in this life if you will pay the price for it. It's up to you. The question is, "Will you persevere? Will you stick to it? Do you have the bull dog determination? Results are waiting. Achievement is just around the corner. But you must not waver; you must not chase rabbits when you are hunting quail."

The Most Critical Time in Your Life

According to Napoleon there is a fifteen-minute period in every battle when the decision will go either way. The General who knows that period and throws everything he has into the battle will win. But the General who does not know it or who is so cautious he will not commit his reserves, will lose not only the battle but inevitably the campaign.

This is the problem in so many lives. People do not know when that critical time is and even if they knew they would not commit everything they have. There comes a time in the shadow of success when you must burn your bridges behind you.

The Romans came to the cliffs of Dover. They first

2 Schwartz, *Ibid.,* pages 80-81.

were repulsed and sent back home. When they came again the Saxons were on the cliffs looking down, far outnumbering the Romans. But the Romans landed and taking all their supplies ashore, turned with one dramatic and decisive event that carried the day. They set fire to their wooden ships and pushed them back out into the English Channel to burn to the waterline and to sink. Then with great resolve they unsheathed their swords and turned to march with forceful resolution into the face of the battle. The Saxons fled. Such persistence, such total commitment was unimaginable. The day was won for the Romans by default.

Do you know when the time is to commit yourself, and are you willing to do it? The results of persistence are yours. There is no way for you to fail. You have learned the law of success and you are challenging that law and demanding that it work for you, not against you. I challenge you to be successful. You can be. The decision is yours.

Persistence Pays High Profits

Persistence is the pile driver that produces the expressway to success:

1. Your major purpose is yours the minute you begin persistent action for its achievement.

   A. List the time needed daily for such action.

   B. State how you will make this the habit of your life.

2. List below Harold Sherman's eight-point pathway to success:

   A.

   B.

   C.

   D.

   E.

F.

G.

H.

3. What changes in your life, business, family, schedule, etc., will you make in order to persistently pursue your purpose?

A.

B.

C.

D.

E.

PART SIX
MOTIVATION

26. WHAT MOTIVATES MEN?

YOUR KEY for success today is that you are motivated by what you believe.

George Elliot[1] said, "We must not inquire too curiously into motives. They are apt to become feeble in the utterance: the aroma is mixed with a grosser air. We must keep the germinating grain away from the light." But experience proves she was wrong. For motives are as vital as our heartbeat. H. W. Beecher hit the truth when he said, "God made man to go by motives and he will not go without them, anymore than a boat without steam, or a balloon without gas." Find what motivates men and we can touch the button, we can turn the key that makes men achieve miracles.

Six Basic Needs

In *How To Live 365 Days a Year, Schindler* lists these six basic needs[2]:

(1) The need for love. There is but one indispensable human emotion and that is tenderness. A person is affected all of his life by the amount of love he received as a child, or the amount he failed to receive. Of course, his romantic love affects him in youth years and in the married years. Certainly, old people must be loved as well.

(2) The second basic need is security. Some psychiatrists believe the child's entire personality is affected if he is weaned too early in life.

(3) The third basic need is for creative expression. Achievement is the tremendously satisfying factor in life. Determine the area you have most talent in and achieve there. You will find great satisfaction.

(4) The fourth need is for recognition. Who wants to be a mere number? Who wants to be only a statistic? This

---

[1]Pseud. of Mary Ann (or Marian) Evans.
[2]Schindler, *Ibid.*, page 198.

organized world tragically submerges the individual into the mob. Recognition, in my opinion, is the most dynamic of all motivating factors.

(5) The fifth is the need for new experiences. One of the satisfying factors of my life has been planning for that next new experience. As soon as I reach one event I immediately set my goal on the next. I like to have engagements months—even years—in advance, and day-dream about those coming events.

(6) The sixth basic need is self-esteem. When we lose our self-esteem we die within. The greatest danger in America today is not the man with the super-ego. The greatest menace is the man with an inadequate ego structure. Recently a survey revealed that 75 per cent of young people entering colleges and 75 per cent of business people applying for work with personnel offices sold their ability short.

Four Principles of Motivation

In the book, *The Magic Power of Emotional Appeal*, the author[3] says that there are four principles of motivation:

1. Self-preservation. This, of course, is the strongest of all. When a man has his back to the wall and his very life is at stake, he will fight with supernatural strength.

2. Recognition. This, is the second most important. No man wants to be a zombie, yet so many are. They've lost their identity—their self-respect.

3. The third principle of motivation is romance. Certainly, when there is romance in a man's work and a romance in his home, his life is dynamic.

4. The motivation of money. And this, in my opinion, is the poorest of all four.

Every man is individualistic. Every man is different. We must learn our man. We must understand him. When we determine which of these motivating principles is most meaningful for him and we turn that key, we can make his life a magnificent obsession rather than a meaningless odyssey.

Goethe said, "If you treat an individual as he is, he will

[3]Roy Garn, *The Magic Power of Emotional Appeal* (Engle-wood Cliffs, N.J.: Prentice-Hall, Inc., 1960), page 20.

stay as he is. But if you treat him as if he were what he ought to be and could be, he will become what he ought to be and could be." The words of the song, "Wishes are the dreams we dream when we are awake," must help each individual to dream at night and wish at day. Men are motivated by dreams, desires, and wishes. Archibald Alexander has said, "Men are more accountable for their motives, than for anything else; and primarily, morality consists in the motives, that is, in the affections."

Motivate Yourself

The emotionally mature man is so much better able to motivate himself than the man of mixed, confused and immature emotions. Some of the things that are important in helping motivation are: the capacity to trust others; the ability to be self-critical; the power of sex ability; a deep sense of self-assurance; and the ability to manage and administer without becoming personally involved in the details of work.

When a man is motivated he achieves. He is successful. His wishes bring forth dedication in his work for he cannot remain on the plain of mediocrity; he must scale the mountains.

Remember the tragic sinking of the atomic submarine, the *U.S.S. Thresher*. How shocked we all were when the reports came out of the shoddy workmanship in building that tremendous submarine—substandard welding, faulty assembly, and poorly soldered electrical connections. As a result of this lack of motivation a hundred men died.

Recently I purchased a sports model automobile. Hardly having driven out of the agency, I discovered the radio would not work properly. The reason—dozens of poorly soldered connections. You see, some mechanic was not properly motivated.

This is carrying over into the tragic drop out of school children. No motivation. Instead of preparing themselves by both high school and college and then technical preparation for a career, many young people are looking just for a job. They learned it from their parents. They got it honestly.

Motivate and Excel

Dr. John W. Gardner, President of the Carnegie Foundation, has said, "An excellent plumber is infinitely more admirable than an incompetent philosopher. The society which scorns excellence in plumbing because plumbing is a humble activity, and tolerates shoddiness in philosophy because it is an exalted activity, will have neither good plumbing nor good philosophy. Neither its pipes nor its theories will hold water."

Properly motivated men are men of purpose and dynamics and dedication.

One of the really outstanding contributions to this study of motivation is by Bob Conklan on his record, *The Key to Motivation.* He says, "It is beliefs, not benefits that truly motivate." To this I agree. Here are some of the questions he suggests that you ask yourself:

1. Are you working for beliefs or benefits?

2. How do you react to criticism?

3. What effect does your belief have on your talents?

4. Does your belief truly motivate?

Bob is right. The man who believes that his work is contributing to the good of others, to the strengthening of society, to the benefit of many other individuals, to the advancement of his own family, and to the strengthening of the principle of Americanism, that man is truly motivated.

"It is beliefs not benefits that motivate." Men are motivated by what they believe. What do you believe? Is the work that you do of blessing to all men your employment touches? If so, you will be a motivated man.

27. HOW TO DEVELOP ENERGY

THIS IS your key for today—develop dynamic energy and you will be successful.

Energy is the ability to act. It is invisible determination, and all healthy people have energy for that which excites them.

Buxton has said, "The longer I live, the more deeply am I convinced that what makes the difference between one man and another, between the weak and the powerful, the great and insignificant, is energy, invisible determination, a purpose once formed, and then death or victory. This quality will do anything that is to be done in the world; and no talents, no circumstances, no opportunities will make one a man without it."

A number of incentives that you might use to energize yourself and your employees are: advancements, awards, challenges, competition, compliments, contests, family award, goals, honor plaques and pins, management development recognition by having employees' names on office doors, superior office furnishings, prestige, prizes, special schooling, special assignments, trips, and happier working conditions.[1] Try these and see how they work with you, for in the final analysis you will have to determine for yourself what works best for each given situation. Remember, every man is different and the factors that energize one man may not move another man at all.

Be an Outgoing Person

Have you ever noticed that truly-energized individuals are emotionally well adjusted? Remember this when you are thinking of the importance of building emotional security in your children. They will be able then to face the trials and tribulations of life. Well-adjusted, outgoing individuals can be hit by the hardest tragedies and yet get up and kick despair in the face as they climb to their feet. You see, they are too interested in others and the world in general to worry about themselves. I've seen such individuals carry their load of burdens for years and yet no one actually knows it's there. They had hidden it in their capacity for energetic action. They have happy, outgoing, enthusiastic expressions. Yes, the energetic person is capable of facing life's storms and calmly sailing through those troubled seas because his eye is on the stars and not on the seas.

In one of his programs of *Our Changing World* Earl Nightingale listed fifteen ways to keep miserable[2]:

(1) Think about yourself. (2) Talk about yourself. (3) Use the personal pronoun "I" as often as possible. (4) Mirror yourself continually in the opinion of others. (5)

---

[1]Edward J. Hegarty, *How To Build Job Enthusiasm* (New York: McGraw-Hill).
[2]*Our Changing World*, No. 676.

Listen greedily to what people say about you. (6) Insist on consideration and respect. (7) Demand agreement with your own views on everything. (8) Sulk if people are not grateful to you for favors shown them. (9) Never forget a service you may have rendered. (10) Expect to be appreciated. (11) Be suspicious. (12) Be sensitive to slight. (13) Be jealous and envious. (14) Never forget a criticism. (15) Trust nobody but yourself.

Now, in order to be energetic and emotionally mature do the very opposite. Think about others. Talk about others. Don't even use the word "I." Do what you know is right regardless of whether anyone agrees with you or not. Don't worry about what others think. Don't care whether they respect you or not. Don't look for such action. If you do, you will never serve others, for you will selfishly want to be served.

When you have completed a service, move on to another. Earn the joy out of the action itself and then forget it has been done. Don't expect to be appreciated. Never let jealousy or envy enter your mind, and acknowledge that a criticism is from a person who needs help and is sick within himself. Pray for such an individual. Exercise kindness. Turn the other cheek toward him and learn to trust everybody, for in so doing you will truly trust yourself. Someone has said, "He that does good for good's sake, seeks neither praise nor award, but he is sure of both in the end."

Here's How to Build Energy

"You have two types of energy. One is physical, the other is mental and spiritual. The latter is by far the more important, for from your subconscious mind you can draw vast power and strength in time of need."[3] Here is the formula for building dynamic energy:

1. Set the goal. Nothing becomes dynamic until it first becomes specific.

2. Keep your body in rigid physical condition. Dr. Thomas Kirk Cureton, Director of the Physical Fitness Laboratory at the University of Illinois, says that a man

---

[3]Napoleon Hill and Clement Stone, *Success Through a Positive Mental Attitude* (Englewood Cliffs, N.J.: Prentice-Hall, Inc., 1960), pages 181-182.

can be as fit at fifty as he was at twenty if he wants to. Dr. Cureton says that a man must first train his whole body and, second, he must push himself to the limit of endurance and exceed the limit with each workout. This then is the art of record breaking—doing more each time than the time before. Therefore enter into a program of physical fitness. Keep your physical body healthy.

3. Eat the right food. By all means take vitamins regularly. At thirty-four I was tired, lacking physical energy. Then I started taking vitamins. At forty I had a lot more energy than I had at thirty-four.

4. Make opportunities to be of service to somebody every day. Practice the Golden Rule. Remember that most people you meet have far greater problems than you have. And never forget that some people can lick their problems if they have a little bit of encouragement, a little bit of kindness.

5. Express your appreciation and kindness to others. Thank the waitress for bringing you the menu. Thank the elevator operator for holding the door or letting you off at your floor. You will be amazed at how this kindness lifts and radiates your day. In 1958 I was on a speaking mission to Yugoslavia. When you enter that country you take your passport to each police station in the village or city that you are in. The police hold your passport until you move on to the next place. In the larger cities it is held at the hotel desk. You leave it when you arrive, you pick it up when you leave. The police check every day, several times a day. In that communistic state they know immediately where you are at all times. I simply treated the communist police as I would anyone, thanking them for their service, smiling in their presence, engaging in conversation through my interpreter, Aaron Jelowich. On each occasion they reflected this kindness. They were gracious to me. I asked my interpreter, "Why?" He said, "Because these people sometimes go for a solid year and never have one kind word said to them. They are so appreciative of your kindness they are kind to you in return." If an atheistic communist wants love, how much more does the person you come in contact with every day!

6. There comes renewed energy in every point of achievement. Remember you are not working for others' praises, you are working because you believe in what you

are doing. And when it's accomplished there is that sweet peace that floods your heart and mind and being.

Energy Unlimited

The greatest discussion of energy that I have found anywhere is in the chapter on energy in Bogardus's *Leaders and Leadership*.[4] An outline of that chapter follows:

1. Application. Work is the steppingstone to leadership. "John Wanamaker shocked Washington when as Postmaster General he came to work at 7:30 A.M. two and one-half hours ahead of official Washington. In 1928, at the age of eighty-two, he was in his office in Philadelphia from 8:00 A.M. to 6:00 P.M."

2. Endurance. Great strength and physique lead to undertaking and accomplishing great tasks."

3. Persistence. "Tenacity of purpose is a quality of leadership. It brooks no discouragement. The harder the game is made, the greater the heights to which the player rises."

4. Courage. "Energy finds expression in an elemental courage that implies leadership. Religious motivation may transform energy into indomitable courage."

5. Assuming Personal Responsibility. "If there is one thing that inspires followship more than another, it is to have someone step out ahead, shoulder a double load, and set the pace. Everyone is also stimulated to assume responsibility."

6. Versatility. "Versatility may keep work and recreation in balanced proportion—versatility keeps a person from getting in a rut. Many positions in themselves require marked versatility."

Develop dynamic energy and you will be a successful person.

[4]Bogardus, *Ibid.*, page 106.

28. MOTIVATION'S SOURCE

YOUR KEY for success today is to develop a projected plan and you will be motivated.

Many people shotgun their motives in all directions, but motivation must be rifled. This is accomplished through a projected plan that scales the heights of achievement.

It's Out of Your Paycheck

The man who is not able to motivate himself must pay his supervisor for doing it for him. Lloyd Conant is quoted by Earl Nightingale as saying, "As long as a person must be supervised, a part of his income must go to his supervisor." That's why the presidents of large corporations make so much money. They are self-motivated. That's why the pay falls off directly proportionate down the line. A part of all the shop foreman's incomes must go to pay the manager and a part of each employee's wages must go to pay the foreman over him.

Frank E. Pfeiffer, President of the Reynolds and Reynolds Company, says, "Management is the means of making things happen and administration is a routine of following certain set procedures whether they produce results or not." Are you a manager or an administrator? True motivation comes when the man has a real dynamic plan of what he is going to accomplish and motivates himself day by day toward the achievement of that purpose.

W. L. Burton, vice-president of sales of the Maritz Sales Builders in St. Louis, Missouri, says, "These following are the standard job inducements: (1) A challenging compensation plan. (2) Sales territories with adequate potential for future growth. (3) Opportunities for advancement. (4) Good products adequately advertised. (5) Prices in line competitively with quality offered. (6) Good service. (7) Sound credit policies. (8) Competent job training and field training. (9) Fair marketing policies."[1]

These job inducements, however, are not the right motivational plans for the best development. Notice the emotions involved in what Mr. Burton calls the eight basic motives that stimulate salesmen to greater effort: "(1) Personal gain. Money, power or prestige. (2) Desire for praise and recognition. (3) Avoidance of monotony and boredom. (4) Pride—job satisfaction. (5) Fear and worry. (6) Desire to be needed. (7) Love of family. (8) Conscience—obligation to others."[1]

Your Plan for Achievement

True motivation comes from a projected plan. Would you try this one on for size:

1. Plot your goal written out in one sentence. Build excitement and satisfaction of the five senses in reaching that goal. It must be primarily of benefit to others. If you set it just for yourself you will never bring the excitement to bear upon it. Remember, greatness is service.

2. Set a year by year checkup with your family and with your business. Plan an exciting, extended vacation with the entire family each year. Get away from the routine. Go to distant places. See interesting things. You will have the joy of anticipating it. You will have the joy of the trip itself. You will have the joy of talking about it and showing the films of it later. Primarily, you will have the joy of doing a wholesome activity with your family.

Check up on the spiritual enrichment of your family. Are you deepening them in the principles of your church? Are you taking them to worship each Sunday?

And now for your business. Are all of the employees enjoying their work? Are they deriving a real sense of achievement in their daily activities? And are you practicing the principles that Lincoln used at the Lincoln Electric Company in Cleveland?

3. Are you building a month by month program of personal achievement? Have you attended Dale Carnegie's course or Napoleon Hill's *Science of Personal Achievement*? Have you gone to a specialized study at a University or some other academic center? Have you given yourself the best possible training for your vocation? Each month check up to see if you are better prepared to do your work than the month before.

---

[1] *Our Changing World*, No. 673.

4. Plan a week by week program of happiness, success and achievement. Plan your week so thoroughly that you will arrive to work on Monday morning eagerly anticipating the next five days. Schedule your activity on Friday afternoon for the following week as Frank Bettger so successfully did to become one of America's outstanding insurance salesmen, a thousand-dollar-a-night speaker and author of so many best-sellers in selling. Schedule your golf game or games so that you are truly recreated. Plan and perform some meaningful hobby, whether it's chess, tennis, bridge, or whatever. Make your week meaningful. And, of course, the most meaningful experience of all is to worship God. Vitally relate yourself to the church of your choice. Become active in it. Join in the character building program for youth. Become a regular and faithful contributor to the cause of your church in its program.

5. Live in day-tight compartments. "Sufficient unto the day is the evil thereof," says the Bible. Let yesterday's problems die with the dusk. If you don't, tomorrow's achievements and opportunities will not rise with the sun. Through playing of outstanding business records, through reading of inspirational books, through your personal devotional life, through your family fellowship, and through your associates at work, you can motivate yourself.

Develop a projected program and you will be motivated.

29. EXCITEMENT

YOUR KEY for success today is dynamic excitement. You can be motivated and successful.

Charles Buxton said, "Experience shows that success is due less to ability than to zeal. The winner is he who gives himself to his work, body and soul." True motivation is fantastically exciting. The motivated man bounces out of bed in the morning, eagerly arrives at work, enthusiastically greets his associates, purposely faces every day's events whether they are problems or successes, finds challenges in every human relationship, and finds personal power to greet every emergency. He is truly a joyful, vibrant, dynamic individual who lives life to the fullest.

One of the interesting facets of communism has been the tremendous exodus of motivated men to the free world. About three million of the best educated leaders, teachers, physicians, scientists, engineers, architects, and other highly skilled specialists have fled to the west. Street signs in Miami today are also in Spanish. Hospital corridors give instruction in Spanish because so many of Cuba's outstanding leaders have fled to the west. The reason—communism does not have the power to motivate men. When men lose liberty they lose motivation. Can the Red world long survive without the dynamics of motivated men?

Get a Glory

Archibald Rutledge tells the story of an engineer on a tiny tugboat crossing a southern river who kept his engine room meticulously clean and went about his work with amazing vibrancy. Asked why he did things so enthusiastically he replied, "Cap'n, it's just this way—I got a glory." If you look on your job of pumping gas in the corner service station as the lower rung toward the presidency of your oil company and the providing of everything you desire for your family and heritage, then you've got a glory. But if you look upon that job simply as making money, then you've lost the glory or you never had it to start with.

Watch Who You Run With

Let me state again: the tremendous importance of developing excitement comes from the people we associate with. We draw emotional strength from the people we are around. If you have a pessimistic friend and you are associating regularly you yourself will be pessimistic. We become what the crowd we run with is. Pick your crowd. Find an excitable, enthusiastic group and draw emotional strength from them.

Also learn to control your bitterness. Nietzsche once wrote, "Growth in wisdom may be exactly measured by a decrease in bitterness." George Washington Carver, the great Negro scientist and outstanding Christian leader, said, "No man can make me stoop so low as to make me hate him." Remember that five minutes of intensive hate burns more energy than eight hours of hard work. Excitement and achievement are directly related to the negative emotions that we've cast aside or learned to rigidly control. Your bank of energy must have regular deposits placed in it. If it does not, you will be overdrawn shortly and the bank will send you a notice. The excitable achiever is constantly filling his bank of energy with joyous, dynamic, purposeful thoughts, associations and moments of inspiration. You have just so much energy to expend. Now use it for your best achievement.

America's First Success Story

Marie B. Ray has written two interesting books that I commend to you: *How Never To Be Tired* and *The Importance of Feeling Inferior*. Let me quote Dr. Ray: "He was born to poverty and became one of the richest men in America. He started life as a printer's devil and became a great writer. He had only two years of schooling and became one of the most learned men of his day. He was of lowly birth and rose to be a first Ambassador to France. He had no training as a scientist, inventor, statesman, and became a leader in all these fields. He was without experience as a courtier and he became the idol of the court of Louis XVI. Benjamin Franklin not only wrote, he lived the first American success story. How did this boy, a nobody and a descendant of generations of nobodies, accomplish this? By a completely honest, a ruthless approach to Ben Franklin, nobody, an unalterable determination to make him a somebody. To that end he launched a direct head-on attack on every liability he possessed with the intention of turning it into an asset.

"His schooling ended at the age of ten. At night, after work, at that age, he studied arithmetic, at twelve he added formal exercises in writing, in his teens he began the study of foreign languages, eventually including French, Italian, Spanish and Latin. He was honored with degrees from Yale, Harvard, William and Mary, even the University of Oxford, in none of which he ever set foot."[1]

---

[1] Marie B. Ray, *The Importance of Feeling Inferior* (New York: Ace Publishing Company), pages 49, 55.

Abraham Lincoln and the Inferiority Complex

Another example of this power of excitement is Abraham Lincoln. No man ever started lower. No man ever had more economic, romantic and political defeats who rose to the height of Abraham Lincoln. What is this factor of dynamic excitement? Marie Ray says it is compensation. She says that there are two ways of compensation— direct and indirect. One consists of turning our liabilities into assets, the other in adopting an overall strategy that leaves the liabilities unchanged and develops other resources to rise above them.

"Without the whiplash of the inferiority complex all talent would lie dormant. It is the spark that disturbs our cloud. For a compensation to be satisfactory and thus allay our painful sense of inferiority, it must fulfill certain conditions. (1) It must be positive, not negative. (2) It must be energetic, not passive. (3) It must be an expression of our own independent thinking and acting. (4) It must be conducive to self-esteem and the esteem of others. (5) It must be socially responsible and valuable. (6) It must give us a normal sense of power and a feeling of goodness."[2]

Here are some of the values of compensation as psychiatrists point them out and as reported by Dr. Ray: "(1) The defective organ or faculty may be trained to function as well as, or better than, the normal one. (2) The function of a healthy organ or faculty may be substituted for the defective one. (3) A situation may be developed in which the defect becomes an advantage. (4) A psychic super-structure may be constructed so that the total personality assumes a pattern which is the compensation for all one's complexes, regardless of their genesis."[3]

People are moved to action by the desire of good and the fear of evil. Which is it with you? Fear or evil will not motivate for very long and the excitement is negative. But a positive, dynamic motivation is the desire for good.

Charles P. Kingsley said, "You have powers you never dreamed of. You can do things you never thought you could do. There are no limitations in what you can do

---

[2]Ray, *Ibid.*, page 59.
[3]Ray, *Ibid.*, page 60.

except the limitations of your own mind as to what you cannot do. Don't think you cannot. Think you can."

30. MOTIVATING YOURSELF AND OTHERS

YOUR KEY for personal success for today is to motivate yourself and then you can motivate others.

The secret of success in motivation is satisfying wants. Therefore, you must first know what your wants are, then you can set up a plan to reach those wants. All actions are the result of motivation. Great deeds come from positive, dynamic motivating factors.

Paul J. Meyer, President of Success Motivation Institute, lists the five symptoms of executive suicide: "(1) Doubt. Doubting yourself and your ability. (2) Procrastination. (3) Devotion to false symbols. Letting symbols become your goals. (4) Complacency. Putting off. (5) Loss of purpose."

The good thing about my friend, Paul Meyer, is that he not only can state a problem but he also has the solution: "(1) Crystallize your thinking. Set a dynamic goal. (2) Develop a plan to reach that goal and give yourself a deadline on its accomplishment. (3) Develop a burning desire to reach that goal. It must become an obsession with you. (4) Develop unshakeable faith in yourself to accomplish it. (5) Create a force of iron will determination. Let nothing keep you from reaching your goal."[1]

Your Mind Can Achieve

The magic ingredient of motivation is hope. Hope is that amazing desire—that dream, that expectancy of realizing what is desired and developing a belief and a plan to attain that goal. We consciously and subconsciously respond to that which is wonderful, desirable, obtainable,

---

[1]Paul J. Meyer, *Who Motivates the Motivator?* Record (Waco, Texas: Success Motivation Institute).

available and reachable. "What the mind can conceive and believe, the mind can achieve." —Stone and Hill.

These hopes come from spiritual, social and personal values. The social worker, the religious worker, the missionary, are motivated to work long and financially unrewarding hours because there is spiritual motivation toward bringing peace and happiness and hope to those they serve. These desires and aspirations are self-generating. They come from within and with each hope achieved, each plateau scaled, others come.

One of the social factors in motivation is status seeking. Now when status can be used for worthy motives to achieve benefit to others, personal satisfaction, good to the family, and be uplifting to the downtrodden masses, then status is wonderful. But, too often status becomes just a symbol—living like the Joneses, owning the company car, the job title, the upper echelon bonus. Then status is corroding and corruptive and ruinous. It is selfish and is no longer social.

Personal values become meaningful when they bring security for our family, assurance of a college education for our children, the necessities of life for aged parents and ourselves, and enough financial security to share our economic achievement with others through the church, social agencies, community fund, etc.

Be a Self Starter

In Nelson Doubleday's personal success program Samm Sinclair Baker has a very fine little booklet on *How To Be a Self-Starter*. Baker's plan of action (page 12) is as follows:

"(1) Study the situation, the need, and the opportunities. Ask yourself, how can I accomplish the most good for my employer, for my family and for myself?

"(2) Tabulate all of the possibilities of action. Count the cost. Evaluate the situation. Study it very carefully. Get all the facts. Write down all the possibilities. Evaluate them.

"(3) Arrange your best possible plan of action. Plan it to minute detail. Bring trusted associates in on your plan. Consider their opinions if they are excitable individuals and can rise to the heights of the motivational appeal that you have used for yourself.

"(4) Re-check the pros and cons. Evaluate before you

start and while you are on your journey. Be quick to plan a program of action; be slow to make changes, but when the overpowering facts necessitate a change never hesitate to admit that you are mistaken. Don't throw good money after bad. Don't throw good hours after bad.

"(5) Take the step. Remember the Chinese Proverb: 'A journey of a thousand miles begins with the first step.' Get at it. The world is watching the man of action."

Let us recall. The principles of motivation are: (1) Self-preservation. This is the most dynamic. (2) Romance. If there is a romance about your job, if there is the romance in your family, if there is the romance, the joy, the exhilaration about all that you do, then life is truly worth living. You are a motivated man. (3) Acknowledge and use the matter of recognition. A motivated man will receive recognition. The successful, dynamic, excited individual is recognized when he walks into a room of strangers. His very step is charged with the vibrancy of success, and he is in a position to motivate and influence others.

Motivation

Motivate yourself and others to be a success:

1. List in order of greatest importance to you the four principles of motivation. Self-preservation, recognition, romance, money.

A.

B.

C.

D.

2. Restate your major purpose. Then add a sentence outlining the use of at least two of the above motivating principles.

3. Grade yourself on the following emotional characteristics, A—Outstanding, B—Good, C—Average, D—Poor, E—Bad:

A. Capacity to trust others—
B. Ability to be self-critical—
C. Power of sex ability—
D. Deep sense of self-assurance—
E. Ability to manage without becoming personally involved—

4. You must develop greater energy to accomplish your purpose.

A. List how you will do so; goals, develop better health, cooperate with others, etc.

B. List your plan to achieve your purpose.

5. List the most exciting individuals you have ever known:

A.
B.
C.
D.
E.
F.
G.

6. Which of their excitable traits do you need the most?

7. How will you develop those traits? Reading, special courses, etc.

PART SEVEN
BUILD BURNING DESIRE AND SUCCEED

31. BURNING DESIRE IS POWER

YOUR KEY to success today is to build a purposeful burning desire.

My dear friend, Craig Jerner, professor of Metallurgy at Oklahoma University, gave me a fascinating book. It is *Incentive Management*,[1] the thrilling story of the success in motivation that James F. Lincoln has used in building the Lincoln Electric Company of Cleveland, Ohio.

For example, in 1956 Lincoln Electric employees' annual earnings were $11,209 while the average for all other manufacturers in America was $4,952. In 1957 Lincoln Electric average earnings were $10,164. The other manufacturers averaged $5,199. In 1959 Lincoln Electric employees earned $10,467 while employees of other manufacturers earned $5,648.

In 1959 the productivity per worker measured by sales dollars for Lincoln Electric was $46,152. The productivity per worker measured by sales dollars for all other manufacturers was $22,075. Why the difference?

Motivation Principles

Mr. Lincoln's first step in developing incentive is to get the desire for cooperation of those involved. A football game is not nearly as involved as is industry with its men, machinery, customers, government interference and taxation, yet industry must develop the same kind of team spirit that a football team achieves in building a tremendous team effort. You have seen teams made up of outstanding stars that never jelled as a team. Consequently they had a losing season when they could have won all of their games, if they had learned to play as a team.

The individual's latent abilities are often brought out by the stress and desire inherent in the game. A specialized

---

[1]James F. Lincoln, *Incentive Management* (Cleveland: Lincoln Electric Company, 1951), pages 80-81, 114-115.

skill that is outstanding will often make a company, as well as a football team, dominate above all others in the field. Mr. Lincoln says, "That desire is what the leader must inspire in all of his organization. The worker must feel that he is recognized in accordance with his contribution to success. If he does not have that feeling of self-respect and the respect of others because of his skill, he will think he is being played for a sucker if he increases his output so that the owners can have more profits."

How is it that an amateur athlete often works as hard or even harder than a professional athlete who is paid for his services? Don't you think the answer is the respect and position that comes from recognition and achievement? Isn't this his reward? "The first problem an industrialist has is to make the job one in which the worker will be proud of his skill and desire to increase such skill," observed Mr. Lincoln.

Briefly, Mr. Lincoln attributes his success to a four-fold principle:

(1) Challenge the worker's ability. Give him something that is beyond his present ability plus a strong desire to accomplish it. Put him into a scrimmage with his fellows to see who is best. Give him the chance to beat the top. In other words, individual challenge.

(2) Make the worker know that there is no limit to his capacities except those that are self-imposed. Jesse Owens did not break the world's record for the broad jump the first time he tried. He would never have approached his best if he had not tried and continued to try to do what he had never done before. He challenged his ability and developed it. All abilities are developed in the same way.

(3) Let everyone know that advancement in the organization comes from within and this advancement depends completely on the ability of those chosen for advancement compared with all others and on nothing else.

(4) Put the development pressure on yourself so that you will develop your own capabilities in making yourself a great leader. You must be the inspiration to your followers. Always expect the impossible from yourself as well as from those around you. You will frequently achieve the impossible if you will but challenge yourself.

Remember the key is to build individual participation and sense of achievement and purpose, and the team play concept that we have on an amateur athletic team. The business—industry—organization—needs to be motivated and unified with the old team spirit that we had in high school and college days.

Fred Smith, one of America's outstanding management consultants, has said, "The difference in a good organization and a bad organization is structure. The difference in a good organization and a great organization is emotional motivation." That's it! Burning desire. Do you have it? Desire is power; you can change your life by building desire.

He Kept on Swinging

Babe Ruth was the world's greatest home-run hitter. He hit a total of 174 home runs and I frankly doubt if anyone will ever measure up to it. But what many people don't know is that Babe Ruth set the world's record for strike outs, too—a total of 1,330. I doubt that anyone will ever measure up to this either but Babe Ruth isn't known for his strike outs; he is known for his home runs. The key was burning desire. He kept on swinging; he never quit.

That's true in the game of baseball, in the work of Lincoln Electric, and in life as well. Remember the words of the Apostle Paul in Philippians 3:14, 15 (RSV): "I press on toward the goal for the prize of the upward call of God in Christ Jesus. Let those of us who are mature be thus minded." Did you get that? The mature person is the one who not only will seek to achieve in this life but will prepare for the next life as well.

Your Biography of Success

In that fascinating book, *The Law of Success,* Napoleon Hill in the section "A Definite Chief Aim," gives a biography of success.[2] Let me list some of these achievements: Woolworth chose as his goal the building of a chain of five- and ten-cent stores. He concentrated on it and did it. Wrigley's was the sale of a five-cent package of chewing gum. It made him millions. Edison concentrated upon the harmonizing of natural laws and he became one of the world's outstanding scientists.

---

[2]Napoleon Hill, *The Law of Success* (Cleveland: Ralston Publishing Company, 1956), Vol. 2, page 50-51.

Henry L. Doherty's goal was the operation of public utility plants. He became a multimillionaire. Ingersoll concentrated on a dollar watch and it made him a fortune. Statler on home-like hotel service and you know of his success. Edward C. Barnes on the sale of Edison dictating machines and he retired as a young man with more money than he needs. Woodrow Wilson set his mind on the White House for twenty-five years and he became its chief occupant. Lincoln, while in New Orleans watching a slave girl being sold, said, "I'm going to hit that traffic and hit it hard." It made him President.

Henry Ford's desire was to make the automobile available to every family in America. He became one of the world's outstanding millionaires. Andrew Carnegie's goal was to lower the price of steel. He became one of the world's richest men. Gillette's desire was to give the entire world a good shave. He became a multimillionaire. George Eastman concentrated on the Kodak and you know of his success.

Russell Conwell's desire was expressed in one address, *Acres of Diamonds,* and it yielded more than six million dollars to philanthropic activities. Hearst built a chain of sensational newspapers. It made him a millionaire. Helen Keller's desire was to learn to speak and she became one of the world's outstanding citizens, a dynamic inspiration to all who know of her story. Marshall Field wanted to build the world's greatest retail store and he saw it in his lifetime. Burning desire is power.

Karl Marx's desire was to destroy capitalism. Lenin desired to bring the world under the control of communism. Beginning in 1903 with seventeen men, in less than fifty years the communists controlled one billion of the world's population. Desire is power. Rightly or wrongly, it is still power.

Take Your Annual Check-up

Did you read the article in *This Week Magazine,* by Dr. William C. Menninger of Topeka, Kansas, entitled, "What a Psychiatrist Would Like to Know About You"? Dr. Menninger tells us that we should take a little time, at least once a year, to check up on where we are going; to see what our goals, purposes, desires are. Dr. Menninger, one of the world's outstanding psychiatrists says that our lives are richer, more meaningful, more purposeful, more dynamic, if we take a regular vacation, if we have useful hobbies, if we can re-create our aims. If your temper is short; if you easily lose control of your emotions; if you find yourself fretting ceaselessly about little things that shouldn't disturb you; then you should get away and in constructive activity—whatever it is you enjoy doing that is re-creative—you can re-structure your goals and desires.

Matton said, "As physicians judge the appetite, judge you by desires." And Cicero has said, "The thirst of desire is never filled, nor fully satisfied." That's what makes desire so powerful. Upon one achievement we move on to greater achievements but desire must be controlled. Certainly, burning desire can be terribly harmful or it can be fantastically successful. You hold the key. You call the signals. It's all up to you. But you ought to make a habit of succeeding.

There's Nothing You Can't Do

"Those things that are not practical are not desirable. There is nothing in the world really beneficial that does not lie within the reach of an informed, understanding, and well protected pursuit. There is nothing that God has judged good for us that He has not given us the means to accomplish, both in the natural and moral world. If we cry, like children, for the moon, like children we must cry on." —Edmund Burke.

Desire is the inward motivating power that propels. Like a fan jet it gives tremendous thrust as the jet shoots forward. Recently I carefully examined a small executive two-engine jet, carrying seven or eight passengers. It has thrust of 5,000 feet per minute, almost straight up— fantastic power. This is but an illustration of burning desire. It will propel you upward to fantastic, amazing success, or the wrong, corroding, corrupting burning desire will drive you down to destruction. It is in your hands. The key is yours to turn.

Our Nation's Biggest Business

Do you realize that education is the biggest business in all of the nation today? Forty per cent of all Americans engage in some sort of educational activity. "There are two-and-a-half million kids in kindergarten; thirty million in elementary schools; eleven-and-a-half million in high school; and four million in college. There are seventeen million people in adult education and nine million in independent self-study," so says Earl Nightingale. Do you realize that this is more than seventy-five million people involved in some sort of educational endeavor? As encouraging as this is, it also means, however, that only 20 per cent of all persons of college age are going to college. What does this say about motivation? Does it suggest that a considerable per cent of these young people simply are not motivated? We are well aware that of the 80 per cent of young people of college age not in college, certainly a group of them are not qualified for college work—either from lack of preparation or by natural endowment. However, it is reasonable to assume that at least 30 per cent of college age young people who are not in college are capable of doing college work. But, you see, they lack burning desire.

In case you are one of these let me build a little desire with these statistics: A man with less than eight years in school earns an average of less than $3,000 a year. The high school graduate, about $6,000 a year. The average income for the college graduate is more than $9,000 a year. This means that the college graduate in his lifetime will earn approximately $150,000 more than the high school graduate. There is another important factor and that is, that the college graduate is prepared in a much larger area of vocational achievement than the high school graduate. He is better prepared to find and to enjoy a place of outstanding service.

The world was shocked some time ago to learn of the terrible effects at birth of a certain drug given to mothers during pregnancy. In London, England, alone 1200 cases of malformation at birth were attributed to this drug. Don't you imagine that the physicians who saw these babies being born, some without arms and legs, some evidently mentally deformed, wondered if they should even start the breath, be true to their oath? But the physicians had no choice, they had given themselves to prolonging life.

146

They Should Have Failed

History tells us of some outstanding examples of people with physical defects, who achieved truly wonderful things. Charles Steinmetz, the electrical inventor who died in 1923, was deformed at birth. He lived to make outstanding contributions to all mankind. There are others who had physical defects—Beethoven, Edison, Julius Caesar, both President Roosevelts, James Ferber, Helen Keller, to name a few. The physical defect was simply another challenge to be successful.

Washington Irving said, "Great minds have purposes, others have wishes. Little minds attain and are subdued by misfortunes; but great minds rise above them." And John Foster said, "When a firm, decisive, spirit is recognized it is curious to see how the space clears around a man and leaves him room and freedom."

Napoleon Hill suggests that burning desire is made up of the following six ingredients: "(1) Self-reliance, (2) Personal initiative, (3) Imagination, (4) Enthusiasm, (5) Self-discipline, (6) Concentration of effort." "Any dominating idea, plan or purpose held in the mind through repetition of thought and emotionalized with a burning desire for its realization, is taken over by the subconscious mind and acted upon through whatever natural and logical means may be available."[3]

"No one has ever been known to succeed without applying the principle of definiteness of purpose. . . . The first step from poverty to riches is the most difficult. It may simplify my statement if I tell you that all riches and all material things that anyone acquires through self effort begin in the form of a clear, concise mental picture of the thing one seeks." —Andrew Carnegie.

My wants are many, and if told,
    Would muster many a score;
And were each wish a mint of gold,
    I still should long for more.
                  —John Quincy Adams

Desire builds desire. This is the fantastic power of it.

---

[3]Napoleon Hill, *Think and Grow Rich* (Greenwich, Conn.: Crest, 1960), page 36.

Your Formula for Burning Desire

The amazing book, *Success Through a Positive Mental Attitude,* gives an explanation of burning desire and how it works.

"(1) ... your subconscious mind begins to work under a universal law: what the mind can conceive and believe the mind can achieve. Because you realize your intended destination, your subconscious mind is affected by this self-suggestion. It goes to work to help you get there.

"(2) Because you know what you want, there is a tendency for you to try to get on the right track and head in the right direction. You get into action.

"(3) Work now becomes fun. You are motivated to pay the price. You budget your time and money. You study, think and plan. The more you think about your goal the more enthusiastic you become. And with enthusiasm your desire turns into a burning desire.

"(4) You become alerted to opportunities that will help you achieve your objective as they present themselves in your everyday experiences. Because you know what you want, you are more likely to recognize these opportunities."[4]

When Charles M. Schwab asked Andrew Carnegie for his first promotion Mr. Carnegie grinned broadly and replied, "If you have your heart fixed on what you want there is nothing I can do to stop you from getting it." That's burning desire.

Five Steps to Success

In his book, *How To Sell Your Way Through Life,* Napoleon Hill lists the five fundamental steps to success: "(1) Choice of a definite goal to be attained. (2) Development of sufficient power to attain one's goal. (3) Perfection of a practical plan for attaining one's goal. (4) Accumulation of specialized knowledge necessary for the attainment of one's goal. (5) Persistence in carrying out the plan."

He also lists some of the advantages of a definite aim: "(1) Singleness of purpose forces one to specialize and specialization tends towards perfection. (2) A definite

---

[4]Hill and Stone, *Ibid.*, page 25.

goal permits one to develop the capacity to reach decisions quickly and firmly. (3) Definiteness of purpose enables one to master the habit of procrastination. (4) Definiteness of purpose saves the time and energy one would otherwise waste while wavering between two or more possible courses of action. (5) A definite purpose serves as a road map which charts the direct route to the end of one's journey. (6) Definiteness of purpose fixes one's habits so that they are taken over by the subconscious mind and used as a motivating force in driving toward one's goal. (7) Definiteness of purpose develops self-confidence and attracts the confidence of other people."[5]

Abe Lincoln Had Purpose

There is no finer example of desire than the life of Abraham Lincoln. Carl Sandburg in his book *Abraham Lincoln: The Prairie Years* quotes the following: "As he walked back to New Salem he saw ahead of him a tough piece of work to do; he had to transform his blank ignorance of surveying into a thorough working knowledge and skill. . . . Many nights (school master) Graham's daughter woke at midnight, and saw Lincoln and her father by the fire, figuring and explaining. Lincoln was fagged, with sunken cheeks and bleary red eyes; 'You're killing yourself,' good people told Lincoln, and among themselves they whispered that it was too bad. In six week's time, however, Lincoln had mastered his books, the chain, the circumferentor, the Three Horizons, and Calhoun put him to work on the north end of Sangamon County. . . .

"Lincoln was challenged to vote for the moving of the capital to Springfield in return for his vote for a measure that he considered against his principles. The debate continued for two days. Then Lincoln spoke: 'You may burn my body to ashes and scatter them to the winds of heaven; you may drag my soul down to the regions of darkness and despair to be tormented forever; but you will never get me to support a measure which I believe to

[5]Napoleon Hill, *How To Sell Your Way Through Life* (Cleveland: Ralston Publishing Company, 1958), page 161.

be wrong, although by so doing I may accomplish that which I believe to be right.' "[6]

Beethoven also had great drive and ambition. Liston to what H. A. Rudall says about him in his biography, *Beethoven*, "Winter and summer, Beethoven rose at daybreak, when he immediately seated himself at his writing table, and continued writing until his usual dinner time at two or three o'clock. His labors were unbroken except for excursions into the open air, but never without a notebook in which to jot down whatever fresh ideas might occur during his rambles."[7]

Houdini, the magician, is another example. Here is a statement from Harold Kellock's, *Biography of Houdini*, "His training for his various immersions, stunts, and feats such as remaining encased in a steel casket under water for an hour and a half were peculiarly arduous. For months on end, several times a day, he would practice going under water in his own bath tub, holding a stop watch to test his own endurance, lengthening the period of immersion each day until he could stay under for more than four minutes without grave discomfort—accustoming himself to get along with a minimum of oxygen, so that he could feed his lungs sparingly with a few cubic feet of air in a little casket and endure for an almost unbelievable time."[8]

Burning desire is a habit and can be cultivated. Success is the progressive achievement of a worthy, challenging goal. You can make the habit of success by developing purposeful burning desire.

[6]Sandburg, *Ibid.*, page 170.
[7]Quoted in *Our Changing World*.
[8]Harold Kellock, *Houdini* (New York: Harcourt-Brace and Company, 1928), page 1.

32. BURNING DESIRE FOR RECOGNITION

YOUR KEY to success today is to build recognition and your burning desire.

Your happiness in life is directly proportionate to your ability to achieve. Achievement brings recognition. Some of the world's greatest people have achieved because of the power of an inferiority complex that thrust them forth to attempt fantastic things to be recognized as individuals.

What do you expect out of life? Do you know where you are going? Are you telling yourself that others will soon sit up and listen to you? That you are fed up with their ignoring you? That you've had enough of no one paying any attention to you and they are going to watch you? Then you are on your way. You are developing a burning desire for recognition.

Depression comes from being ignored. It is tragic to be just a face in the crowd. So stand out from the crowd. Set a big goal in whatever area you can best achieve in, a goal that will acknowledge you as an outstanding successful, dynamic individual. You are on your way to personal success when you do so.

Remember, as a child, reading the first circular about the circus coming to town? Remember how you anticipated going to a baseball game? Remember how you looked forward to the first swimming experience of the summer? Yes, you lived for weeks on that one dream. Now you must do the same thing as an adult. You must set a tremendous goal out there and develop your desire to reach it, because that goal will lead you to personal happiness. In the achieving of it you bring about the recognition your conscious mind desires and must have.

One of the human relations rules that has made the Dale Carnegie Course so powerful is, *Throw down a challenge*. The "well done" of the boss, your name in the company newspaper, a human interest story in the daily paper about you, the spoken admiration of friends and

151

associates, as well as the anticipated, "Well done thou good and faithful servant" of the Lord—all are means of thrusting people forward.

A Sense of Confidence

Many times we need external aids to buoy up our spirits, our moods. Clothes and external conditions can be controlled to a great extent by our own attitudes and conduct. One amazingly successful automobile salesman who specializes in selling luxury cars to wealthy individuals tells of his formula for success in Bristol's *The Magic of Believing*. "Not only do I take a shower," he said, "and change all my clothes, but I go to a barber shop and get everything from a shave to a shampoo and a manicure. Obviously, it has something to do with my appearance, but further than that it does something to me inside. It makes me feel like a new man who could lick his weight in wildcats."[1]

In one of his challenging radio programs entitled *Consciousness of Competence*, Earl Nightingale discusses the secret of success of the outstanding star, whether he be in athletics, show business or in the business world. Earl says that there are three facts: "(1) Each of these stars is in the work which comes the closest to perfectly matching his natural talents. He's where his abilities lie. (2) These people are dedicated totally to what they are doing. Everything else takes second place in their life. (3) They have supreme confidence. They can assault their work with boldness, with assurance, with confidence because they know they can succeed."

I have seen men in combat with that same sense of assurance. In fact, toward the latter part of the Okinawa campaign I had a little bit of it myself. The vast majority of my friends were either killed or wounded in combat; yet I wasn't touched. It was almost a fatalistic sense of assurance that whatever happened I would come through it all right. My name simply wasn't written on one of those bullets.

Novalis said, "Happy those who here on earth have dreamed of a higher vision. They will the sooner be able

---

[1]C. M. Bristol, *The Magic of Believing* (Englewood Cliffs, N.J.: Prentice-Hall, Inc., 1948), page 167.

to endure the glories of the world to come." And Thomas Carlyle said, "There is no man, no woman, so small but that they cannot make their life great by high endeavor."

> I held a truth, with him who sings
> To one clear harp in divers tones,
> That men may rise on stepping-stones
> Of their dead selves to higher things.
> —Alfred Tennyson

Thought on Fire

Burning desire will reflect itself in fiery words. William Jennings Bryan defined eloquence as, "The speech of one who knows what he is talking about and means what he says—it is thought on fire. . . . Eloquence is when a speaker is tremendously enthused about worthwhile things concerning which he is thoroughly informed."

Furthermore it is impossible to achieve true recognition without service to others. The greatest recognition is in the individual heart when we know what we have done—what we've given our life to—that has lifted up the down-trodden, given hope to the distressed, and encouragement to the downcast.

Dr. Kenneth McFarland, possibly America's greatest after dinner speaker, in his book *Eloquence in Public Speaking* quotes the following, "Dr. Edward Rosenow, formerly with the Mayo Clinic in Rochester, Minnesota, told of the experience that caused him to become associated with the field of medicine. When he was a small boy living in Minnesota, his brother became acutely ill. The family sweated it out until the doctor arrived. As the physician examined his sick brother, Edward Rosenow kept his eyes riveted on the anxious and anguished faces of his parents. Finally, the doctor turned to his parents with a smile and said, 'You can relax, folks, your boy is going to be alright.' Young Edward Rosenow was profoundly impressed with the change that announcement brought over his parents. In relating the incident in later years he said, 'I resolved then and there that I was going to be a doctor so I could put light in people's faces.'"[2]

---

[2]Kenneth McFarland, *Eloquence in Public Speaking* (Englewood Cliffs, N.J.: Prentice-Hall, Inc., 1961), page 31.

That's it. That is true recognition. And let me say that the burning desire is there when you wish to be recognized for the service you have rendered to others, not necessarily external recognition but internal recognition of a job well done—of putting light in people's faces, of easing the pain of a troubled heart, of giving purpose to a wasted rascal, of bringing harmony to a broken home, of giving joy to a troubled boy.

Is Anything Really Impossible?

"We all have possibilities we don't know about. We can do things we don't even dream we can do. It's only when necessity faces us that we rise to the occasion and actually do the things that hitherto have seemed impossible." — Dale Carnegie. "Life does not consist mainly—or even largely—of facts and happenings. It consists mainly of the storm of thoughts that is forever blowing through one's head." —Mark Twain. We must corral those thoughts, direct those thoughts, harness those thoughts toward our recognition.

"I desire so to conduct the affairs of this administration," said Abraham Lincoln, "that if at the end, when I come to lay down the reins of power, I have lost every other friend on earth, I shall at least have one friend left, and that friend shall be down inside of me." This is the internal recognition that desire brings to reality. Winston Churchill said the same thing when he said, "So long as I am acting from duty and conviction, I am indifferent to taunts and jeers. I think they will probably do me more good than harm."

Henry Ford said, "All Fords are exactly alike, but no two men are just alike. Every new life is a new thing under the sun; there has never been anything just like it before, and never will be again. A young man ought to get that idea about himself; he should look for the single spark of individuality that makes him different from other folks, and develop that for all he's worth. Society and schools may try to iron it out of him; their tendency is to put us all in the same mold, but I say, 'Don't let that spark be lost; it's your only real claim to importance.' "

"There is a time in the lives of most of us when, despondent of all joy in an earthly future, and tortured by conflicts between inclination and duty, we transfer all the

154

passion and fervor of our troubled souls to enthusiastic yearnings for the divine love, looking to its mercy, and taking thence the only hopes that can cheer—the only strength that can sustain us." —Edward George Bulwer-Lytton.

Build Burning Desire and Succeed

Burning desire is the jet propulsion to success:

1. You will need others to help you achieve your major purpose. List the individuals and groups who will help you build burning desire.

2. Make a list of the most exciting, enthusiastic individuals you have ever known, or heard about. Try to name at least 20.

3. List below the books you must get to help you establish a consistent program of improving your burning desire. (Start with the Bibliography at the back of this book.)

4. Through victory over worry, association with vibrant people, an ever improving program of creative study, and the regular statement of your burning desire, you will make a habit of succeeding. List your next immediate action to achieve burning desire.

33. HOW TO ACHIEVE BURNING DESIRE

YOUR KEY for success today is to make the habit of succeeding and achieving. You must develop burning desire to achieve an outstanding purpose that will motivate and unify the total powers of your being.

In one of his programs from *Our Changing World* Earl Nightingale gives a formula for making a million dollars:

"(1) Get into a line that you will find to be a deep personal interest, something you really enjoy spending twelve to fifteen hours a day working at, and the rest of the time thinking about.

"(2) Learn all you can about this line, and what everybody else in the same line is doing, especially the more successful ones.

"(3) Submit yourself completely. That is, surrender yourself to this one line then make up your mind to succeed at it.

"(4) Develop patience. Realize that one of the most important ingredients of success is realizing how long it takes to succeed. In fact, you must be in your line a minimum of five years, and be solidly in the black by that time, to even be considered successful. Most real success will come back to the first five years.

"(5) Learn to ignore the unimportant and distraction. You've only got so much time, make sure you use it to its best advantage.

"(6) Create, don't compete. Think ahead and move with intelligent boldness into new and perhaps unexplored areas of development. Lead, but don't follow."[1]

Excellent advice by a master of success. This then is your formula for succeeding. You can be successful. It's all up to you. You call the signals of your life.

There is no short cut to achievement. There are many who would think that the only way to excell is by pull or by fraud or by someone in a high place recommending you. Even if you get the position you can't hold it unless you have mastered the principles of success; unless you know the field thoroughly; unless you can match any and every other man of equal position not only in your firm, but among all competitors as well. Actually, pull may be the worst thing that could happen to a young man trying to succeed. It can destroy.

Kate Smith didn't have pull. Here was a young woman with everything going against her. She didn't know anyone to recommend her, she was large but she had a great voice. It took her many years to get started, but she had

---

[1]*Our Changing World*, No. 892.

the nation applauding her. You see, you can't stop burning desire. If your desire is strong enough you will achieve.

A word of caution from Matthew Henry: "Inordinate desires commonly produce irregular endeavors. If our wishes be not kept in submission to God's providence our pursuits will scarcely be kept under the restraints of His precepts." Be sure that your burning desire is the right one—that your goals are God's goals.

How to Change the Business Pattern of a City

Years ago I shopped at a store whose motto was, "The store that will never know competition." The owner-manager, who had been trained at Marshall Field in Chicago, had a burning desire to change the mercantile habits of a metropolitan area, and he did exactly that by the magic of competition and the motivation of advertising. He not only lowered prices, produced jobs, developed a competitive spirit among merchants, but directly and indirectly, his influence brought dynamic new life to an entire city. He had a burning desire to achieve.

Climb on the Bumps

Nothing can stop the man who has this desire to achieve. Eric Butterworth, in *Good Business Magazine*, tells the following story: "A little boy was leading his sister up a mountain path. She complained, 'It's not a path at all. It's all rocky and bumpy.' 'Sure, the bumps are what you climb on.'" Nothing stops the man who desires to achieve. Every obstacle is simply a course to develop his achievement muscle. It's a strengthening of his powers of accomplishment.

Did you hear about the boy in Decatur, Illinois, who answered an ad in the magazine about a book on photography, but received a book on ventriloquism instead? He kept the book, studied it, made a wooden dummy to practice with and became internationally known. That's right, Edgar Bergen and Charlie McCarthy. He took the bump of disappointment and stepped on it to a highway of success.

Don't be like the boy during World War II who said, "I wouldn't mind going to war and being a hero if I knew I wouldn't get hurt." The hurts of life's journey are but the exercise bar of achievement. They are the push-ups to outstanding success.

When General Dwight Eisenhower addressed the troops before Normandy, he said, "There is no victory at bargain basement prices."

Is there a more thrilling story of desire and purpose in achievement than that of Florence Nightingale? It was impossible for her to find a hospital in Britain that would train her to be a nurse so she might go to the battlefield and meet the needs of wounded soldiers. She went to Germany and there served an apprenticeship in want and embarrassment. Early in the Crimean War she literally changed the whole world's concept and attitude toward caring for the wounded in military battles. Upon her deathbed when more than ninety years of age, Florence Nightingale in a semiconscious condition was heard to say, "I am watching the altar of murdered men, and I shall be eternally fighting their cause."

How to Stay Young

Bristol quotes one outstanding man who, though beyond seventy, gives the following secrets of success: "I make it a plan, and have for years, to start something new—that is, new for me—at least, once a week. It may be only the making of some simple gadget for use in the kitchen or it may be an entirely new sales plan or reading an unfamiliar book. I find in following this plan not only that I keep my body and mind active, but also put to use a lot of imaginative qualities that otherwise might fall asleep and atrophy. This idea of man's retiring when he is sixty is to me a great mistake. As soon as a man retires and quits being active mentally and physically he is on his way to his grave in short order. You've seen what has happened to fire horses when they are retired. You know what happens to an automobile when you leave it outside unused and neglected; it starts to rust and it's soon headed for the junk shop. Humans are the same; they rust out or wither and die when they go on the shelf."[2]

---

[2]Bristol, *Ibid.*, page 153.

Your Driving Force of Destiny

The reason burning desire is so necessary in success is that we put forth the effort directly proportionate to the power of emotionally exciting ourselves to achieve. Desire is the driving force of destiny. Desire can accomplish amazing feats.

What are you striving for? Where are you going? Do you know? You cannot begin to build burning desire until you plan the program, until you establish the purpose, until you outline the goals—the road signs along the fabulous journey of dynamic purpose—and in this you must expect to achieve.

You realize there are two types of energy, one is physical and the other is mental and spiritual. Now the mental and spiritual energy is far more important, for a subconscious mind can bring forth great power and strength whenever needed.

How He Broke the Four Minute Mile

Dr. Roger Bannister broke the four-minute mile for the first time on May 6, 1954.[3] Dr. Bannister believed, along with his trainer, that it was necessary first to mentally assent that he would break the four-minute mile. Then his body could be developed to the point of physical perfection to accomplish this outstanding feat. Not only did he do it, but just four years later on August 6, 1958, five runners ran the mile in less than four minutes in one race in Dublin, Ireland. In those same four years the four-minute mile was performed forty-six times by Bannister and other runners.

The man who taught Roger Bannister this secret was Dr. Thomas Kirk Cureton, Director of the Physical Fitness Laboratory of the University of Illinois. Dr. Cureton says that any man can be as fit at fifty as he was in his twenties if he knows how to train his body. He says that a few principles are involved: (1) To train the whole body. (2) To push yourself to the limit of your endurance exceeding the limit with each workout. The art of record

---

[3]Hill and Stone, *Ibid.*, page 182.

breaking is the ability to take more out of yourself than you've got. You punish yourself more and more each day you practice.

According to Your Desire

"We believe that according to our desire we are able to change the things round about us, we believe this because otherwise we can see no favorable solution. We forget the solution that soon comes to pass and is also favorable; we do not succeed in changing things according to our desire, but gradually our desire changes. . . . We have not managed to surmount the obstacle, as we were absolutely determined to do, but life has taken us round it, led us past it, and then if we turn round to gaze at the remote past, we can barely catch sight of it, so imperceptible has it become." —Marcel Proust.[4]

"Whatever I have tried to do in this life, I have tried with all my heart to do well; whatever I have devoted myself to, I have devoted myself to completely; in great aims and in small, I have always been thoroughly in earnest." —Charles Dickens.

"Perseverance is power to weakness, and opens to poverty the world's wealth. It spreads fertility over the barren landscape, and bids the choicest fruits and flowers spring up and flourish in the desert abode of thorns and briars." —Samuel Goodrich.

Take Possession of Your Mind

Andrew Carnegie said, "The man who acquires the ability to take full possession of his own mind may take possession of anything else to which he is justly entitled. . . . And the man who masters himself through self-discipline never can be mastered by others."

It cannot be burning desire unless it builds fantastic determination.

"I'll not budge an inch." —Shakespeare.

"The best lightning rod for your protection is your own spine." —Emerson.

"He who is firm and resolute in will molds the world to himself." —Goethe.

---

[4]Marcel Proust, *Remembrance of Things Past* (New York: Random House).

"Either I will find a way, or I will make one." —Sir P. Sidney.

"Energy will do anything that can be done in the world; no talents, no circumstances, no opportunities will make a two-legged animal a man without it."—Goethe.

"The truest wisdom, in general, is a resolute determination." —Napoleon.

"Toil—zeal—think—hope; you will be sure to dream enough before you die, without arranging for it." —Sterling.

You must build in your mind's eye a fantastic desire, a burning desire to achieve, to excel. As a man thinkest in his heart so is he.

Earl Nightingale quotes Dr. Leslie J. Nason, a professor at the University of Southern California. "You can read a child's image of himself in his actions. If he thinks he's tough it shows. If he thinks he's afraid, it shows. If he thinks he's good, it shows. If he thinks he's bad, it shows. You see, he develops this image of himself in the same way we all do, by seeing how others react to what we say or do. The parent establishes the image by telling the child, that he is always misbehaving or that he is a fine little boy. The teacher in school brings out the best in the good students, or brings out the worst in the unruly students by continuing to comment on it time after time after time. But most of all we act like the person we think that we really are. It's up to us. Everyone must have some kind of a personal image to guide his behavior. It usually causes trouble only when it is wrong." These truths by Dr. Nason are so evident. But, you can change the image you've had in the past. You can make your mind do what you want it to do. You can achieve, provided you build a burning desire.

34. BURNING DESIRE DEVELOPS COMPETITION AND PRIDE

YOUR KEY for success today is developing competition and pride.

Earl Nightingale tells about a man who was observed

running toward a large river. As he reached the dock he increased his speed and when he came to the end he threw himself as high and as far out as he could before hitting the water, landing about ten feet from the dock. As soon as he surfaced he swam back to the land and tried it again, over and over again. A friend asked him "What are you doing?" He said, "A friend of mine has bet me a million dollars to one that I can't jump across the river and after thinking over those odds, I couldn't help at least trying." This is competition. The spirit of competition, of courage, and of personal pride is one of the outstanding emotional factors in the achievement of the American way of life.

The 25 per cent of the salesmen who make 75 per cent of all the sales succeed because they continue to stay at the job. They do not give up. They have courage and a sense of competition. Competition is to contend with another for a prize, to engage in a contest, to compete in a race or in business or in any activity, to strive to outdo, to excel as an individual or a group of individuals. It implies a sense of rivalry in striving to give one's best in outdoing others. Certainly there is the suggestion of opposition and disputing, as well as rivalry. There are obstacles to overcome. There is personal discipline involved. There is struggle and hard work and fear and frustration and friendly enemies to overcome. Charles F. Kettering has said, "I have found that if I have faith in myself and in the idea I am tinkering with, I usually win out." Now notice the sense of competition; Kettering was competing with possible scientific failure and with other businessmen. He had a goal; he had a purpose; he had a plan.

You Are Stronger Than You Think

Dale Carnegie has said, "We can all endure disaster and tragedy, and triumph over them—if we have to. We may not think we can, but we have surprisingly strong inner resources that will see us through if we will only make use of them. We are stronger than we think." William James said, "To feel brave, act as if you were brave, use all of your will to that end, and a courage fit will very likely replace the fit of fear." Ralph Waldo Emerson said, "They can conquer who believe they can. He has not learned the first lesson of life who does not every day surmount a fear."

How many times have you held off attempting a certain thing because you simply knew it couldn't be done? You had made up your mind ahead of time. Then for some reason you were forced to try and you soon realized that from a distance that which seemed impossible soon was easily accomplished, and you could have kicked yourself for not attempting it sooner.

Develop Competition

A spirit of healthy competition developed in the home with children when they are young, exercised and challenged on the athletic field and in the classrooms, then brought to fruition and richness in the business corridors of adult life brings joy, accomplishment and intensive achievement.

Did you hear about the boy who was such a problem, getting into everything, that his father suggested they buy him a bicycle for Christmas, and the mother said, "Will that make him any better?" The father replied, "No, but it will spread his devilment over a wider area." The rambunctious, dynamic, devil-may-care boy is not the one you usually need to be worried about. However, I'm not suggesting that you tell such a boy to sit still while you instill. You just don't say to a ten- or twelve-year-old boy, "Don't do this or don't do that or don't move." You simply wiggle him in the right direction. He is already competitive. He has a yen for life.

The child to be concerned about is the child who is an introvert—the wall flower type, the afraid-of-his-shadow individual. He doesn't relate and he doesn't compete. Lee H. Oswald, the murderer of President Kennedy on November 22, 1963, was a loner; he did not relate.

When you get a kid out of his shell and get him to compete he begins to live. He is a part of the effort and he's beginning to bring forth his best, the totality of his ability in competition. The same thing happens to the tragic number of high school dropouts—no competition. Never forget that the man who with his college or graduate degree thinks he has the world as his own is already a failure, for he has ceased to compete. An education is to give a man a tool or to tell him where he can find the tool to make life's decisions and to meet life's emergencies and to scale life's mountainous opportunities. The man who has been educated beyond his intelligence is the one who's sitting on top of his degree and is self-satisfied.

Your Well-Integrated Personality

Have you read Dr. Alexis Carrel's book, *Man, The Unknown?* He says "that the individual who succeeds has an intensity that determines the social level of that individual and that the happiest and most useful persons are those with a well integrated whole of intellectual, moral and organic activities. ... The so-called genius, the great artist, the great scientist, the great philosopher, the great musician, the great business success, is generally a man of common ability who has overdeveloped one particular phase of his abilities and personality." So he says, "Genius can be compared to a tumor that is growing upon a normal organism."

But do you know that many of these people are unhappy? They give to the entire community the benefit of their mighty impulses, but they often are disgruntled, in disharmony and out of step with other people. Yes, Dr. Carrel says, "The happiest people and the ones making the greatest contribution to life are those with well integrated personalities." In other words, they relate to others and respond to the challenge of others in a spirit of competition that brings forth a burning desire.

You have far greater ability than you ever dare believe. Remember, the average person uses less than 10 per cent of his total mental capacity.

What a terrible excuse I used to give myself in arguing against the learning of memory techniques to improve my capacity to memorize. I would say, "You can only remember so much so if you crowd out things you've already learned then you won't have room for all you need to know." How foolish. The most fertile field in all the world and the greatest unexplored territory in all the universe— even greater than space itself—is the human mind. You learn to use every tool you can to strengthen your mental powers. Develop this sense of competition. You will find that out of it will come a greater desire to accomplish, to achieve, to stand above the crowd.

Stay Competitive and Achieve

Such a spirit of competition is what someone has well

called, *designed discontent.* Remember those lines of Joel Chandler Harris: "Watch out w'en you'r gittin' all you want. Fattenin' hogs ain't in luck." The competitive man is never satisfied. He never ceases to grow; he never stops learning; he never stops achieving; he moves on from one area of achievement to another; on and on and on.

Recently there was a newspaper article telling about certain businessmen who through heavy schedules had come to times when they needed to relax and were forced by doctor's orders to take a leave of absence from their business to go away to rest. An amazing thing was discovered. These men simply weren't pleased, weren't content, weren't happy to do nothing. While they were away on a ninety-day leave it was discovered that they had started a new business, taken on the consulting for another firm, or opened up a hotel or whatever. The article went on to summarize by concluding that there are certain men who have superior bodies and superior minds and superior abilities. They actually are superior men. Were they born that way? No, they achieved through competition and pride and burning desire.

> Greatly begin! though thou have time
> But for a line, be that sublime—
> Not failure, but low aim is crime.
> —James Russell Lowell

> Aspire, break bonds, I say;
> Endeavor to be good
> And better still, and best—
> Success is nought, endeavors all.
> —Robert Browning

There was a day in our world when a gentleman was a man of wealth and of leisure who owned such vast pieces of property and, in some eras, slaves, that all he had to do was count his coupons and live a life of luxury and leisure. Isn't it wonderful that that has changed? A gentleman today is a man who treats other men as if they were better than himself or at least his equal.

Burning Desire in a Single Pursuit

Remember those days at the high school track meet and running those sprints in your football uniform at practice?

Remember those joyous summer games of seeing who could dive the greatest distance or swim under water the furthest; of seeing who could throw the baseball the furthest? That's what we need to continue to do—develop the spirit of competition. And when a man has done his best, has given his all, and in the process supplied the needs of his family and his society, that man is successful—that man has made a habit of succeeding.

The person who will seek to get something from someone else without paying due process for what he receives also has never learned the joy of competition. It is just as much stealing to take pay for work not done or not completed as it is to hold a pistol to a man's brow. Estimates are that four million dollars in cash and merchandise is stolen from employers every day in America. This means a billion dollars a year—a tragic indictment. What terrible proof that men have not learned the true joys of competition and burning desire.

Earl Nightingale quotes Milton Carlton, who as an eleven-year-old won a speech contest in a California school. Let me repeat his words, "In speaking of men who've made outstanding success, 'They had a burning drive to succeed; they refused to accept failure as the final answer; they often turned physical handicaps into assets; they had concern for other people; and they worked hard and constant. There is very little difference in people—that little difference makes a big difference. The only difference is attitude. From the time we are in kindergarten, we've heard the story about the little engine that climbed the hill by saying, "I think I can—I think I can." ' " What a speech by an eleven-year-old boy!

Yes, competition is the key to burning desire and burning desire is the joy of achievement. Remember you can do anything in the world you want, if you can build a burning desire. Make your contest a joyful, happy, gracious one. Let your competitors be your friends; build a spirit of wholesome competition and you will find that life is truly worth living. You can make a habit of succeeding.

35. PRODUCING BURNING DESIRE

YOUR KEY to success today is to produce burning desire and make a habit of succeeding.

What man can conceive mentally, he can bring into materialization. Regardless of how depressed you may be, you can restore burning desire immediately by returning to the goals and the purpose to which you dedicated yourself originally. Never forget that the persistent achievement of a worthy challenging goal is success.

In his marvelous book, *Eloquence in Public Speaking,* Dr. Kenneth McFarland, one of America's outstanding public speakers, says that "the indispensable quality to speaking as well as to leadership is vitality." This word is found to mean "of critical importance, of truth, imparting life and vigor, animation, living, fundamental, essential, important, significant, necessary, needful, exuberant, something having vital force." "It contains enthusiasm, along with truth and other life-giving qualities that insure the proper direction of enthusiasm."[1]

Here's How

You can produce burning desire. Let me give you a formula: First, you must have a goal; and of course, goals are purposes. Goals and purposes differ only in degree. Purpose is the long range, all encompassing dream of your life; goals are check points along the road to success. Do you know where you are going? Do you know what you want to do? Remember, we become what we think about. If you have a goal, you have a personal image. If you have a goal you live and breathe and walk and act with dynamics and with purpose. If you see the man on the street hurrying, head back, shoulders erect, with military bearing, forcefulness of action, there is a man with a goal.

[1]McFarland, *Ibid.,* page 238.

He knows what he is doing. No coward can be a crusader.

Napoleon Hill said, "Any idea that is held in the mind, emphasized, feared or reverenced, begins at once to clothe itself in the most convenient and appropriate physical form that is available."[2] And Hill also says, "The transfer of thoughts from the conscious to the subconscious section of the mind may be hastened by the simple process of stepping-up or stimulating the vibrations of thought through fear, faith, or any other highly intensified emotion, such as enthusiasm, that is, a burning desire based on definiteness of purpose."

Christopher Columbus dreamed of a new world and set out to achieve it regardless of the cost. We know what happened. Thomas A. Edison dreamed of lighting the world with incandescent lamps and he worked on his dream incessantly. Though he paid the price of 10,000 failures he gave the world light. Samuel Johnson said, "Our desires always increase with our possessions. The knowledge that something remains yet unenjoyed impairs our enjoyment of the good before us."

The second way to produce burning desire is to renew our dynamic energy. Never allow ourselves to get stale. Remember Dale Carnegie: "Is giving yourself a pep talk every day silly, superficial, and childish? No—on the contrary. It is the very essence of sound psychology." Keep excited about your work. We are excited when we are earnestly following a pathway toward a glorious, romantic, and eager achievement that is out before us. Take the ten-year-old boy who hears about a circus coming to town. He's excited.

People become stale because of several facets: too much work, or too much play, or no routine of activity, or failure to have and find balance in life. Man is a fourfold being. He is physical; he is mental; he is social; and he is spiritual. Therefore your daily and weekly activities should include creative mental stimulation. It is very important that you find this in your work. The man who dies a little bit during eight hours of work is dead at home as well.

Certainly there should be the stimulation of joyous and meaningful social intercourse, the building of new rela-

---

[2]Hill, *Master Key to Riches*, page 61.

tionships with other individuals and the sustaining and strengthening of existing relationships. Of course, everyone needs a program of physical fitness and physical improvement and all of us are spiritual beings and need a daily and weekly worship relationship. Choose the church of your choice and throw yourself into it vitally. There is no such thing as communing with God in the country, at the lake fishing, or on the golf course, or in the garden. It is impossible. Through all of your life must run the joy of service.

The third way to produce burning desire is to stay competitive in your work. Cultivate and continue the joy of achievement and the spirit of competition between others involved in the same general vocation. The man who quits studying, the man who quits reading, the man who quits working, dies in his business at that time. People often say to me, "When do you find time to read?" We find time to do the things that we want to do and that are meaningful to us. I read on the plane and waiting in the doctor's office. I read at every moment, those inbetween moments that so many people waste. I read late at night after the day's responsibilities while others are watching the meaningless program on television. Observe what is good; take part in that which is meaningful on television; but practice the discipline of rejecting that which has no plan or purpose in your life.

The fourth thing is to regularly congratulate yourself on your achievements. Count your blessings. Realize that you are working toward your goal, that you are achieving.

The fifth way to produce burning desire is to be creative. To do this you must push yourself. You have great and unlimited ability—ability that has never been challenged, ability that has never been extended. In some colleges and universities 75 per cent of the freshmen flunk out. Isn't this tragic? They couldn't have entered with present day examinations if they did not have the ability to finish. But they were not creative; they didn't challenge themselves; they did not set out to achieve.

I have a friend who has a doctor's degree but the minute he received it he quit learning. He is stagnated today. Tragically and corrosively he has limited his life and those round about him. He failed to be creative.

There are certain companies who have a policy only to hire college graduates. Certainly there are fields that require specialized training that only a college degree can give, but some of the most outstanding individuals this world has ever known were those who were thrust forth into dynamic action from the sense of inferiority that a lack of complete education gives. Personally, I'd rather have an enthusiastic, dynamic individual who is creative and wants to achieve, with a limited education, any day than a man with all the degrees in the world who is through learning.

Dr. John W. Gardner, President of the Carnegie Foundation, says that the American people are placing an altogether false emphasis on college education. He feels that great prestige which the college degree has achieved in our society leads people to assume—quite incorrectly—that college is the only form of continued learning after high school. Learning is for life and if you are to produce burning desire you must continue to be wonderfully creative.

You can make a habit of succeeding by producing burning desire!

How to Achieve Burning Desire

Making a habit of burning desire assures you of success:

1. Forget your inferiority complex and with bold commitment restate your major purpose.

2. Take Earl Nightingale's formula for making a million dollars and apply this six-point plan to your major purpose.

    A.

    B.

    C.

    D.

    E.

    F.

3. List the disappointments of your life that now you realize were the bumps on which you climbed to success.

4. Take the so-called impossible situation in your life and with Roger Bannister's formula outline your record breaking goal.

    A. Train your whole body. How?

    B. Push yourself to the limit each day exceeding the workout before. Now apply it to your situation.

5. Remember Bannister first decided mentally he could do it. You can too. Outline your plan to take complete possession of your mind.

6. Achieve desire by:
    A. Stating your goal.

    B. Renewing your dynamic energy. How?

    C. Staying competitive. How?

    D. Congratulating yourself on your achievements. Now you are great—say so.

    E. Being creative. How?

PART EIGHT
NOW — ACTION!

YOUR KEY for success today is planning—planning that achieves.

An architect spends many hours with a client determining the dreams, goals, purpose, intents and uses in the heart of the client for the building. He literally picks the mind of the client. Then he puts these aspirations on paper with proper drawings and specifications so that the contractor, sub-contractor and all suppliers can perform their function properly to achieve the ideal building.

Your road to success requires planning. You must make plans, think about them, act on them.

Action is as essential to success as the motor and fuel are to the auto. But results are the only excuse for activity. We must know why we are acting and act toward the fulfillment of our goals.

Andrew Carnegie, who amassed a fortune of $500,000,-000, said, " 'Knowledge is power' is only a half truth, for knowledge is only potential power. It may become a power only when it is organized and expressed in terms of definite action. Knowledge is not power, but the appropriation and use of other men's knowledge and experience for the attainment of some definite purpose is power."

A Chinese proverb says, "Journey of a thousand miles begins with first step." But in what direction? Plan your direction. When the goal is clear, the purpose is strong, the step will be decisive, assertive and forceful. Direction and determination decide destiny.

Make Big Plans Now

Daniel Hudson Burnham said, "Make big plans. Aim high and hope and work, remembering that a noble, logical diagram once recorded will never die, but long after we are gone will be a living thing, asserting itself with ever-growing insistency. Remember that our sons and grandsons are going to do things that would stagger us."[1]

Proper planning can save your life. In 1953, I started using auto safety seat belts. In March 1961, a farmer drove onto the highway, never stopping and hit me on the left side as I was driving seventy miles an hour. I turned over six times, completely demolishing the car. The car landed upside down in a drainage ditch. I walked away with only a minor wound on my forehead and spoke four hours later. I owe my life to planning.

One Thing Needed

There are many things that go to make up success: good health (not always essential), energy—a product of good health, perseverence, common sense, enthusiasm, talent. However one thing has been left out of that list—the one thing without which all of the others cannot produce success. That thing? Work. Work that is coordinated with what we want to accomplish. Another word we might use for work is action.

A circus had advertised that they had twenty-four elephants. On the day of the parade a busy executive on his way to his office was caught by the parade. He must not miss his appointment which meant hundreds of dollars in commissions. He remembered the advertisement of twenty-four elephants. As the elephants came into view the trunk of one holding onto the tail of the one in front, he decided to count to twenty-four and gun his car across between the last elephant and the next vehicle. He counted, nineteen, twenty, twenty-one, twenty-two, twenty-three and as the trunk of the twenty-fourth came into view he gunned his car and shot across the intersection. What he did not know was that they had brought one more elephant. He hit the elephant, killed it and wrecked his car.

The circus manager and police arrived. They said, "You'll have to pay."

The businessman answered, "It's my fault, I'll pay, how much?"

"Thirty-five thousand dollars."

"What? You can get an elephant delivered from Africa

---
[1]*Our Changing World*, No. 795.

for five thousand dollars. All I did was kill one elephant."

They exclaimed, "No, it isn't, you killed one elephant and pulled the tail out of twenty-four more."

The man in the story had a plan and acted on it. But he did not check his plans thoroughly and it cost him money. Failure to investigate and prepare for all emergencies can happen in our world too.

Make big plans and act on them. Check up on them regularly. You can be successful.

37. PROPER ATTITUDE

YOUR KEY for success today is the proper attitude. Your success is determined by your attitude. The fruits of success—sense of achievement, peace, exhilarating keen competition, etc.—will not be yours unless your view toward your desire, achievement, success, is right. There must be an inner satisfaction that what you are doing is what you should be doing, that you are doing what you can and all you can. This then helps to motivate you. Your attitude determines your action.

> Let me be classed with the highest or lowest,
>   Only with these will the senses be keen,
> You'll either find me the fastest or slowest.
> I'll never rot with the dull in between.
> —Jack Wardlow

In his book, *The Story of Man*, Carleton I. Coon says, "Hunting exercises the whole body, as few other occupations do. It places a premium on keen eyesight. Farsightedness is an asset. Hunting also places a premium on the capacity to make quick decisions, to act quickly and to work in teams. Obedience and leadership can be developed at no better school."[1]

---

[1]Carlton, I. Coon, *Story of Man* (New York: Knopf, 1962), page 47.

We are hunters, on that glamorous, romantic, intriguing hunt of success. There are prices to pay, rivers to cross, mountains to climb, incurring loss of sleep and other difficulties, but the anticipation of the hunt, the fellowship and exhilaration of the occasion and the delightful hours of continual discussion will many times benefit the hunter.

The Golden Key — Initiative

"Initiative is that exceedingly rare quality that prompts —nay, impels—a person to do that which ought to be done, without being told to do it." —Napoleon Hill. Elbert expressed himself on the subject of initiative in these words, "The world bestows its big prizes, both in money and hours, for one thing and that is initiative. Initiative is doing the right thing without being told."

Enthusiasm is the lubricant that oils the machinery of action. Each person has varying amounts of energy, depending on capacity for excitement, worthiness of the goal, associations around you and other factors.

Learn to store, utilize and expend your energies to your best advantage.

Five minutes of hate expends more energy than eight hours of hard work.

You can greatly improve your personality by changing your attitude. Control of temper, stern discipline of hate, jealousy, and revenge with insertion of positive thinking, love, hope, desire can make your life a magnificent obsession rather than a meaningless odyssey.

38. ACTION DEVELOPS COURAGE

ACTION REQUIRES courage. But action also develops courage. You can be successful. Do you have the will to believe? Do you dare to walk by faith? Do you have the capacity to gather information rapidly, yet thoroughly, and then to act? An executive is one who can act.

The common attitude among so many people is: don't stick your neck out—don't get out on a limb. Many people are afraid to get out on a limb and they haven't even climbed the tree yet. Right after World War II people said, "Don't build. The cost is too high. Prices will go down." And for the next six years costs went up at approximately 1 per cent per month. They could have saved fabulous amounts of money had they built when the need was there—right after the war.

Georges Clemenceau said, "A man who likes to be convinced to act before he acts is not a man of action. Do you see the tennis player before returning the ball begin to question himself as to the physical and moral value of tennis? You must act just as you breathe." And Oliver Wendell Holmes, Jr., said, "Life is action and passion; therefore, it is required of a man that he should share the passion and action of his time at the peril of being judged not to have lived."

Make Your Own Inspiration

Great men do not wait for inspiration. The curse of action is the thought that we have to *feel* a certain matter before we act. There is nothing in this world as fickle as feeling. Our emotions are governed by our volition and follow volition. Forget emotions! Let's act.

Professional writers laugh when someone says, "I have to wait for the mood. I must court the muse and wait for inspiration." You'll never make a living writing if you do that. There are deadlines to be reached. Furthermore, the more we write, the more the inspirational material rises, for action stimulates the thought processes, brings from the subconscious the real truth and the greatest inspiration. If you act you will find that you will accomplish far more than if you wait needlessly.

Would you like to have more courage? Dale Carnegie gives five short rules, which, if you follow them, are guaranteed to increase your fortitude.

"(1) Act as if you were courageous. This makes you a bit braver, as if one side of yourself had been challenged and wished to show it was not wholly afraid.

"(2) Pause to reflect that others have had to face great discouragements and great obstacles and have overcome them. And what others have done, surely you can do.

"(3) Remember that your life forces move in a sort of rhythm and as you feel depressed without the power to face life you may be at the bottom of your trough; if you will keep up with your courage, you will probably swing out of it by the very forces which at the moment are sucking you down.

"(4) Remember you feel more discouraged and downcast at night than during the daylight hours. Courage comes with the sun.

"(5) Courage is the measure of a big soul. Try to measure up."[1]

Action Cultivates Your Own Courage

So well do I remember combat in the Pacific in the Marine Corps during World War II. If you stayed in your foxhole and worried about being shot, you would either lie there in fright and frenzy or crack up emotionally. You got out of that foxhole. You acted. And with the increased action day by day courage came. General Omar Bradley had said, "Bravery is the capacity to perform properly even when scared half to death." Bravery requires action and with action there come other responses as well.

It was Dale Carnegie who said, "I've never felt sorry for anyone, man or woman, for having to earn a living. I do look with inestimable pity, however, on anyone who has no enthusiasm for the type of work he is doing. To me, it is a great tragedy if one does not find early in life the kind of work he likes to do that he may apply in full force all the enthusiasm of youth." "If you are devastated by sorrow, by disaster or calamity, get busy doing something. Keep your mind and your hands occupied. To do this will help you as nothing else will. I know. I have tried it."[2]

In private flying I've learned that action drives away fear. It is common practice that when a person cracks up a plane, the best thing for him to do is to go up again as soon as he is physically able. This drives away fear.

Have a Fireside Talk With Yourself

In the dark days of the depression there was fear as thick as fog clouding the minds of so many Americans.

---

[1]Dorothy Carnegie, ed., *Carnegie's Scrapbook* (New York: Simon and Schuster, Inc., 1959), page 6.
[2]Carnegie, *Ibid.*, page 193.

President Roosevelt called Napoleon Hill to his office in 1933 and discussed with Mr. Hill a plan to restore calm to a troubled people who had lost confidence in themselves and in their nation. Mr. Hill tells that the motto chosen was, "One for All and All for One." It was set up to cross all political party lines. All communications media, all radio, newspapers were brought in on the team. Instead of business depression they would talk about business recovery. The public schools at all levels were a part of the project. The clergy of all denominations were encouraged to preach on the positive rather than the negative. Then President Roosevelt began his series of fireside chats in a warm, friendly, folksy manner that brought tremendous confidence. We all know the answer. Almost immediately the nation began to think positively. And it began to move economically. Yes, courage follows action.

Don't you like the words of the Russian proverb, "Pray to God, but keep rowing to the shore"? Someone has said that "We ought to pray as if all depends on God, but we ought to work as if all depends on us." Courageously you can be successful.

39. ACTION PRODUCES ACHIEVEMENT

YOUR KEY for personal success for today is action, for in action there is achievement. And achievement is success. You can be successful. The man of success is the man of action. Theodore Roosevelt said, "I took the canal zone and let Congress debate, and while the debate goes on the canal does also." Teddy Roosevelt—a man of tremendous action and courage.

Action brings achievement. Earl Nightingale has come up with a formula that suggests that a person's net worth is sixteen and two-thirds times his annual salary. What is your average annual income? Multiply that times sixteen and two-thirds and you will come up with the amount you are worth. You may have earned twice that figure, of course, in your lifetime but your present cash value is sixteen and two-thirds times your annual income. If you make $10,000 a year you are worth $156,666, that is, if you are a man of action. But if you aren't a man of action you aren't a man of achievement. Phillips Brooks says, "Do not pray for tasks equal to your powers; pray for powers equal to your task. In the doing of your work shall be no miracle, but you shall be the miracle."

Prison Set Him Free

Clement Stone and Napoleon Hill tell the challenging story of action by Kenneth Erwin Harmon, a civilian employee of the Navy at Manila when the Japanese landed there in 1941. He was captured and held in a hotel for two days before he was sent to prison camp. There in the prison camp he saw a book that a cellmate had. It was entitled, *Think and Grow Rich*. He read it. He became infatuated with it and then asked the friend if he could copy it and the friend said yes.

He began feverishly, word by word, page by page, chapter by chapter, night and day, constantly knowing that soon they would be separated and he would no longer have the book. Within an hour after the last page was completed he was transferred to the notorious Santo Tomas prison camp in Manila where hundreds and thousands of prisoners of war died. All during the more than three years of imprisonment he read all and memorized much of *Think and Grow Rich*. At the end of the war when he was released, he had no fear of the present or the future. His words are, "But I was better when I left Santo Tomas than when I was interned, better prepared for life, more mentally alert. Success must be continually practiced or it will take wings and fly away."[1]

Action brings wonderful, glorious, outstanding achievement. You can be successful. The decision is yours.

Now — Action!

Action seals the habit of succeeding:

1. Since a major purpose well stated is half-achieved, restate your major purpose in progressive tense.

---

[1]Stone and Hill, *Ibid.*, pages 94 and 95.

I am continuing to achieve ...

2. Fight failure with action by taking Earl Nightingale's ten reasons why people fail[2] and stating your positive solution. (The first solution is done for you.)

A. "Ignorance of the law of success."
   The law of success is the persistent achievement of a worthy, challenging goal and I've got mine.

B. "Inability to concentrate on what is important."

C. "Lack of organization."

D. "Stop learning."

E. "Loss of faith in yourself."

F. "Cling to status quo."

G. "Custom is king."

H. "Do as little as you can get by with."

I. "Never evaluate yourself."

---

[2] *Our Changing World*, No. 567.

J. "Give up."

3. Since genius is the capacity for taking infinite pains, state 9 more details of your journey to success.

Begin every day stating my major purpose to myself.

4. The Golden Key is initiative: What move are you going to make—NOW?

BIBLIOGRAPHY

BOOKS

Albert, Dora. *You Are Better Than You Think*. Englewood Cliffs, N.J.: Prentice-Hall, Inc., 1957.

Allen, Mel and Graham, Frank, Jr. *It Takes Heart*. New York: Harper, 1959.

The Amplified Bible. Grand Rapids, Mich.: Zondervan Publishing House, 1965.

Baker, Samm Sinclair. *Your Key to Creative Thinking*. New York: Harper, 1962.

Battista, O. A. *The Power To Influence People*. Englewood Cliffs, N.J.: Prentice-Hall, Inc., 1959.

Bettger, Frank. *Benjamin Franklin's Secret of Success and What It Did for Me*. Englewood Cliffs, N.J.: Prentice-Hall, Inc., 1960.

————, *How I Multiplied My Income and Happiness in Selling*. Englewood Cliffs, N.J.: Prentice-Hall, Inc., 1954.

————. *How I Raised Myself From Failure to Success in Selling*. Englewood Cliffs, N.J.: Prentice-Hall, Inc., 1958.

Brande, Dorothea. *Wake Up and Live!* New York: Pocket Books, Inc., 1939.

Bristol, Claude M. *The Magic of Believing*. Englewood Cliffs, N.J.: Prentice-Hall, Inc., 1957.

Bristol, Claude M. and Sherman, Harold. *TNT: The Power Within You*. Englewood Cliffs, N.J.: Prentice-Hall, Inc., 1954.

Bryant, Al. *1,000 New Illustrations*. Grand Rapids, Mich.: Zondervan Publishing House, 1957.

Carnegie, Dale. *How to Stop Worrying and Start Living*. New York: Simon and Schuster, Inc., 1948.

————. *How To Win Friends and Influence People*. New York: Simon and Schuster, Inc., 1936.

Carnegie, Dorothy, ed. *Dale Carnegie's Scrapbook*. New York: Simon and Schuster, Inc., 1959.

Custer, Dan. *The Miracle of Mind Power*. Englewood Cliffs, N.J.: Prentice-Hall, Inc., 1960.

Davidson. Clinton. *How I Discovered the Secret of Success in the Bible*. Westwood, N.J.: Fleming H. Revell Co., 1961.

Doan, Eleanor. *The Speaker's Sourcebook of 4,000*. Grand Rapids, Mich.: Zondervan Publishing House, 1960.

Edwards, Tryon, ed. *The New Dictionary of Thoughts*. New York: Standard Book Company, 1957.

Ely, Virginia, ed. *I Quote*. Westwood, N.J.: Fleming H. Revell Co., 1963.

Flesch, Rudolf. *The Book of Unusual Quotations*. New York: Harper, 1957.

Gabriel, H. W. *Twenty Steps to Power, Influence, and Control Over People*. Englewood Cliffs, N.J.: Prentice-Hall, Inc., 1962.

Garn, Roy. *The Magic Power of Emotional Appeal*. Englewood Cliffs, N.J.: Prentice-Hall, Inc., 1960.

Germain, Walter M. *The Magic Power of Your Mind*. rev. ed. New York: Hawthorne Books, Inc., 1956.

Giblin, L. T. *How To Have Confidence and Power in Dealing With People*. Englewood Cliffs, N.J.: Prentice-Hall, Inc., 1956.

Giniger, Kenneth S., ed. *The Compact Treasury of Inspiration*. rev. ed. New York: Hawthorne Books, Inc., 1964.

Gorman, Mike. *Every Other Bed*. Cleveland: The World Publishing Co., 1956.

Haggai, John Edmund. *How To Win Over Worry*. Grand Rapids, Mich.: Zondervan Publishing House, 1959.

Hart, Hornell. *Autoconditioning*. Englewood Cliffs, N.J.: Prentice-Hall, Inc., 1956.

Hegarty, Edward J. *How To Build Job Enthusiasm*. New York: McGraw-Hill Book Company, Inc., 1960.

————. *Showmanship in Public Speaking*. New York: McGraw-Hill Book Company, Inc., 1952.

Henry, Louis C. *Five Thousand Quotations for All Occasions*. Garden City, N.Y.: Garden City Books, 1956.

Hill, Napoleon. *How To Sell Your Way Through Life*. Cleveland: Ralston Publishing Company, 1958.

————. *The Master-key to Riches*. Los Angeles: Willing Publishing Company, 1945.

————. *Think and Grow Rich*. rev. ed. Greenwich, Conn.: Fawcett Publications, Inc., 1960.

Hovey, E. Paul. *The Treasury for Special Days and Occasions*. Westwood, N.J. Fleming H. Revell Co., 1961.

Howard, Vernon. *Success Through the Magic of Personal Power*. Englewood Cliffs, N. J.: Prentice-Hall, Inc., 1961.

Laird, Donald A. and Eleanor C. *Tired Feelings and How to Master Them*. New York: McGraw-Hill Book Company, Inc., 1960.

Lincoln, James F. *Incentive Management*. Cleveland: Lincoln Electric Company, 1951.

McCay, James T. *The Management of Time*. Englewood Cliffs, N.J.: Prentice-Hall, Inc., 1959.

McFarland, Kenneth. *Eloquence in Public Speaking*. Englewood Cliffs, N.J.: Prentice-Hall, Inc., 1961.

Maltz, Maxwell. *Psycho-cybernetics*. Englewood Cliffs, N.J.: Prentice-Hall, Inc., 1960.

Martin, Clement G. *How To Live To Be A Hundred*. New York: Frederick Fell, Inc., 1963.

Milt, H. and Stevenson, G. *Master Your Tensions and Enjoy Living Again*. Englewood Cliffs, N.J.: Prentice-Hall, Inc., 1959.

Murphy, Joseph. *The Power of Your Subconscious Mind*. Englewood Cliffs, N.J.: Prentice-Hall, Inc., 1963.

Narramore, Clyde M. *Improving Your Self-Confidence*. Grand Rapids, Mich.: Zondervan Publishing House, 1961.

―――――. *This Way to Happiness*. Grand Rapids, Mich.: Zondervan Publishing House, 1958.

Peale, Norman Vincent. *The Power of Positive Thinking*. Englewood Cliffs, N.J.: Prentice-Hall, Inc., 1954.

Price, Eugenia. *What Is God Like?* Grand Rapids, Mich.: Zondervan Publishing House, 1960.

Prochnow, Herbert V. *The Public Speaker's Treasure Chest*. rev. ed. New York: Harper, 1964.

Prochnow, Herbert V. and Herbert V., Jr. *A Dictionary of Wit, Wisdom, and Satire*. New York: Harper, 1962.

Roth, Charles B. *My Lifetime Encyclopedia of Selling Ideas*. Englewood Cliffs, N.J.: Prentice-Hall, Inc., 1963.

―――――. *Winning Personal Recognition*. Englewood Cliffs, N.J.: Prentice-Hall, Inc., 1954.

Sadhu, Mouni. *Concentration*. New York: Harper, 1959.

Schindler, John A. *How To Live 365 Days a Year*. Englewood Cliffs, N.J.: Prentice-Hall, Inc., 1955.

Schleh, Edward C. *Successful Executive Action: A Practical Course in Getting Executive Results*. Englewood Cliffs, N.J.: Prentice-Hall, Inc., 1956.

Schwartz, David J. *The Magic of Thinking Big*. Englewood Cliffs, N.J.: Prentice-Hall, Inc., 1959.

Sherman, Harold. *How To Turn Failure Into Success*. Englewood Cliffs, N. J.: Prentice-Hall, Inc., 1958.

Starch, Daniel. *How To Develop Your Executive Ability*. New York: Harper, 1943.

Stone, W. Clement. *The Success System That Never Fails*. Englewood Cliffs, N. J.: Prentice-Hall, Inc., 1962.

Sweetland, Ben. *Grow Rich While You Sleep*. Englewood Cliffs, N.J.: Prentice-Hall, Inc., 1962.

―――――. *I Can, The Key to Life's Golden Secrets*. New York: Cadillac Publishing Company, 1953.

―――――. *I Will!* Englewood Cliffs, N.J.: Prentice-Hall, Inc., 1959.

Uris, Auren. *How To Be a Successful Leader*. New York: McGraw-Hill Book Company, 1953.

Walker, Harold Blake. *Power To Manage Yourself*. New York: Harper, 1955.

Whiting, Percy H. *The Five Great Rules of Selling*. rev. ed. New York: McGraw-Hill Book Company, 1957.

RECORDS

Bennett, Millard. *The Power of Inspired Salesmanship*. Waco, Texas: Success Motivation Institute, Inc.

Brown, Ralph R. *The Power Within You*. St. Louis, Mo.: Sales Success Unlimited.

Clasen, George F. *The Richest Man in Babylon*. Waco, Texas: Success Motivation Institute, Inc.

Conklin, Bob. *The Key to Motivation*. Minneapolis, Minn.: Midwest Audio-Visual Company.

Conwell, Russell. *Acres of Diamonds*. Waco, Texas: Success Motivation Institute, Inc.

Kohe, J. Martin. *How To Overcome Discouragement*. Waco, Texas: Success Motivation Institute, Inc.

Leterman, Elmer G. *Personal Powers to Creative Selling*. Waco, Texas: Success Motivation Institute, Inc.

Ling, Mona. *How To Get Appointments by Telephone*. Waco, Texas: Success Motivation Institute, Inc.

Meyer, Paul J. *Who Motivates the Motivator?* Waco, Texas: Success Motivation Institute, Inc.

Nightingale, Earl, *Lead the Field*. Chicago, Nightingale-Conant, Inc.

———. *The Strangest Secret*. St. Louis, Sales Success Unlimited.

———. *The Top Five Percent*. Chicago, Nightingale-Conant, Inc.

Steincrohn, Peter J. *Mr. Executive: Keep Well — Live Longer*. Waco, Texas: Success Motivation Institute, Inc.

Sweetland, Ben. *I Can*. Waco, Texas: Success Motivation Institute, Inc.

Wardlaw, Jack. *Thought Plus Action*. Waco, Texas: Success Motivation Institute, Inc.